Diplomacy and Persuasion

Diplomacy and Persuasion

How Britain Joined the Common Market

Uwe Kitzinger

Thames and Hudson · London

Printed in Great Britain by
The Camelot Press Ltd,
London and Southampton

ISBN 0 500 01080 3

Contents

List of Tables and Diagrams

Acknowledgments

For typing a voluminous correspondence and the bulk of the text I should like to thank my secretary, Margaret Bett, and for helping to take the overload at crunch week-ends also June Harris of Standlake.

To Harriet Macandrew, my research assistant until April 1972, I owe vast files of press cuttings and also the computer breakdowns set out in the Appendix 1; her successor Dov Zakheim read the popular press and tabulated the opinion polls. I am grateful to both for checking innumerable details, for holding the fort during my frequent absences, for their patience with me, and for their unfailing support. Thanks are also due to John Hawkins who drew the graphs, and to John Goulding who prepared a difficult typescript for the printer.

For permission to reproduce the opinion polls set out mainly in Chapter 12 and Appendix 3, I am grateful to the Opinion Research Centre and Louis Harris Research Ltd, Social Surveys (Gallup Poll) Ltd and NOP Market Research Ltd.

My greatest debt of all is due to the Warden and Fellows of Nuffield College. It is just ten years since I became one of their number. I could not have hoped for a happier comradeship of endeavour.

The friends who were neglected, burdened with portions of the draft, or both, shall remain nameless. It is to the closest of them that the book is dedicated.

For Sheila

Preface: Some Headaches of Contemporary History

Seek not to present a perfect work
The Lady Julian of Norwich

This is a tale of three cities: Paris, Brussels and London. It is made up of several strands. In Franco-British relations it starts at the nadir with the Soames affair – when French civil servants found it difficult to accept even dinner invitations at the British embassy – and ends with the Queen's visit to Paris, welcomed by President and people alike. Over British entry into the EEC it starts with Harold Wilson's conversion to accession to the Rome Treaty, and ends with his fight in the House of Commons against an alien system of law. In British domestic politics it begins with the difficulties faced by the newly elected Conservative government and the danger for the Conservative Party of splitting over the Common Market: it ends with a deep rift in the Labour Party over the issue, with the government on that issue happily in the clear. In the realm of public opinion and its formation, it begins with a 71:12 majority in favour of entry in 1966 and via a 17:63 majority against entry in 1971 ends with a more balanced but still unfavourable division of view. It describes both the Goliaths of the hidden and overt persuaders in favour of entry, and the embattled Davids fighting their tactical rearguard action against, from which a strategic counter-offensive may yet emerge.

Several of these themes thus have their own dramatic unity. Others, however, form part of the continuing themes of British politics: the reassessment of Britain's role in the world, the up and down (and stop and go) of her economic tides of fortune, the conflict between tradition and modernization in the Conservative Party, between Left and Right, and between Parliamentary Party and trade unions on the Labour side. These strands implicitly run through the story as the continuing warp that began long before it, and may well continue – changed and conditioned, no doubt, by these events – into the future.

To that extent what this book seeks to describe is certainly a test case in the political process, but also one that is too atypical to constitute a representative example. Even if it is not representative, however, it can be an exception that 'proves' the rule: the working of the British political system in unusual circumstances can serve to throw unusual light on its normal nature. Moreover, the events described in this book undoubtedly have to be regarded as sufficiently special to be worth remembering historically for their own sake – and for the way they may prove to have affected the future of the system. What the book does not attempt to do explicitly is to sort out which are the general rules, which the particular accidents. That is a task which it is in many ways too early for either historian or political scientist to perform – which is why the book ends without any presumptuous attempt at a chapter of summary 'conclusions'.

One could, of course, have waited another six months, until more people had been interviewed, more alleged facts cross-checked, more points of view considered. One could have waited four or five years, until the memoirs of some of the principal present actors begin to sprout on the bookshelves. (Those of Harold Wilson, George Brown, Couve de Murville and some other actors in the 1967 attempt are already available.) One could have waited thirty years, when the official archives will allow us to distinguish in detail the attitude of a key civil servant in one week from his reactions three weeks later. One could wait until, at some as yet indeterminate date, some major phase of European integration appears to be concluded, then to put Britain's entry and subsequent events into historical perspective. At each of these points the story will have to be re-written, no doubt from different points of view. With each re-writing it will become more complete in one sense – but also perhaps less 'true' in another.

The present essay thus does not set out to be a cathedral. It constitutes at most a quarry. (The fact that Marketeers and anti-Marketeers alike may use stones from it to throw at one another is a different matter.) The cathedral – if it can ever be accomplished – will have to be constructed with stone from many quarries. Moreover, this particular way of telling the story will no doubt provoke the publication of further material. In that sense it is itself a tool of research, a means for others to gather further material before it is too late, for future treatment in more traditional historical style or future use in more systematic political analyses.

The contemporary chronicler – and the bulk of this book was written in early 1972 – certainly has some advantages over the traditional historian; but he also faces in particularly acute form problems which impinge rather less on those writing of a remoter period. Four problems in particular have troubled me, and on each of them I owe the reader some kind of explanation of what I have tried to do. The four problems are those of objectivity, of reliability and completeness of evidence, of 'political discretion', and of the chronicler's own concept of the structure of political events. The four problems tend to become intimately intertwined.

Classical historians either spontaneously see, or more consciously reinterpret, events of a previous epoch in terms of their own images of the world as it is or ought to be. The contemporary chronicler or political analyst would have to be a peculiar creature indeed if he were at once sufficiently interested to work in detail on public events and yet devoid of any personal views on those events or on the political framework in which they take place. I happen to have been an advocate of world-wide and hence also European political integration since my schooldays, and an active participant on the side of the 'Marketeers' for many years. Rather than pretend to any impartiality, to which I would lay little claim, I can only warn the reader of my open bias. As one of my informants put it: 'On this issue, silence would have been the only neutrality.'

This bias obviously affects the overall framework in which I see the story. It would be understandable for an anti-Marketeer to wait before recounting the same events until Britain has re-extricated herself from this monstrous Continental entanglement. For him 1 January 1973 cannot be a natural terminal point for a sub-division of the story, but only the most farcical episode in it. Nonetheless, I hope that before too long there will be an account of these events written from the opposite point of view to set against mine. In turn, of course, both points of view may seem irrelevant, or beside the real point, to historians or political scientists dealing with the same period but with a different focus.

The reliability of the evidence in writing an almost immediate chronicle is not necessarily less than in the more classical forms of writing. Some of my worst sources have been published ones. Some of my best informants have been my friends. Yet memory is fallible. A colleague recalls having been given by five informants four different names for the chairman of an important meeting.[1] I have also met strident contradictions and, given the limitations on time to triple-check information, I have no doubt succumbed to unnecessary and painful

[1] David Butler and Michael Pinto-Duschinsky, *The British General Election of 1970*, Macmillan, London, 1971, p. xiii.

inaccuracies. But in addition I have, for example, had categorical denials from different sources of the presence or involvement of a certain civil servant in one set of events, a certain politician in another, a certain diplomat in a third – each denial countered from other sources with detailed descriptions of their behaviour or regularity of attendance; and I have had written denial of four statements in international minutes from the man responsible for these minutes, which will no doubt form a source for the classical historian. Some of the means of checking will become available to later historians, others will be irretrievably lost to them. Our work, once again, is not so much competitive as complementary.

It is on the completeness of the evidence that the contemporary historian – certainly when he is dealing with as complex and international an event as this – inevitably falls short of the classical. I have interviewed several hundred people and read several thousand press reports, but am conscious of having had to leave untapped a great many further possible sources. It will be apparent that I have interviewed widely in London, a good deal in Paris, a little in Brussels, and not at all in Bonn, Rome, The Hague, Washington or other relevant cities. This was for obvious logistic reasons. My thanks go to all who were willing to give me of their time and counsel, quite a few of them by writing memoranda or commenting on draft chapters no less than by long conversations. It is part of my thanks, particularly to some of those to whom I am most grateful, that I mention none of them by name.

This leads to the consideration of my third problem – that of political discretion. Almost inevitably any contemporary chronicler knows more than he feels he can tell. Some facts are acquired by being oneself involved in events, and are therefore not available for use in a different capacity. Some facts are given off the record for academic purposes as background material to help interpretation but not for use. Some facts are supplied for use but only on condition that their source cannot be identified – but it then proves impossible to state the facts accurately in such a way as to obscure the source. Some facts are not given but obtrude themselves within a context of implicit confidentiality.

These are the easy cases. But there are other facts specifically given to me for use on the record, either immediately or else after a certain lapse of time, the publication of which might, however, itself affect either the further progress of the events described, or the actors in them, or even other historians' access to future information. In some cases the repercussions would most probably be trivial, while the historical relevance of the events is appreciable; in others the detail may be incidental to the story, while repercussions on those involved might be unhappy. These are not simply questions of balancing probabilities: in these cases issues of principle arise. On the one side is the role of academic work in relation to the long-term development of the polity as a whole; on the other, the personal loyalties and the immediate political causes in which any individual academic happens to be involved. The separation of personal from professional life is a general problem of social role in which there are general standards, however ill-defined, both as to the use of information and as to the treatment of individual cases (including one's personal friends) in an impersonal fashion. It is here that the privileges of academic life impose their heaviest responsibilities.

The problem arises both in that part of the story which concerns diplomacy and in that concerning domestic persuasion. How far, in either case, does one go in the naming of civil servants who played important roles, and did so for reasons and in ways which showed them clearly to be rather more significant individuals than mere interchangeable cyphers doing no more and no less than executing their political masters' bidding? How relevant on the domestic side is the exact source of a sum less than £5,000 spent on a particular public relations exercise?

How far does one go – on the diplomatic side of the story – in tracing disagreements between the Permanent Representation of the French Republic in Brussels, different schools of thought in the Quai d'Orsay, and thinking in the Elysée? To what extent and in what detail is a 'conflict' or 'difference of emphasis' within the British official machinery on French intentions, or on tactics of co-operation with the so-called 'friendly five' rather than with the French, a fit subject of anecdote and of comment? How relevant to the establishment of a tactical line by the British delegation was a conversation between two civil servants in a taxi or the absence of a Minister in Mexico at a certain moment? How crucial was a particular dinner in a Brussels restaurant attended by French and British delegates? How far in fact is anything that happens at an official meeting ever decisive – or even at the unofficial preparative meeting or in telephone calls before these – compared with the plans laid in his study or while driving to the office by the man whose ideas happen on that occasion to be adopted? Is it not in this private rumination or where two or three cabal together that the roots of history lie? It is here that the questions of discretion mingle with those of the level of historical and political discourse, as it reflects both the detail of the evidence available, the minutiae to which one can subject a reader and – more important – the underlying catagories of causality in decision-making.

More and more as I look at the political process – and this is even truer for international political processes than for national ones, a point that many would no doubt think of major topical political importance – it turns out to be constructed like Peer Gynt's onion. There will be history books in the future which sum up the four hundred pages of this volume in the four words 'Britain joined in 1973 . . .'. In so doing they will with perfect accuracy portray the blue outer skin of the onion. Sir Con O'Neill has been writing an official history for the Foreign Office considerably longer than this book, which deals it would seem essentially with the topics here sketched in a mere two or three chapters. Long newspaper articles have already appeared about, and future memoirs will deal in massive chapters with, topics here skated over in a paragraph or so. This book sets out to deal with the middle layers of the onion.

But it is not really the level of description that raises the problem, uneven as it has to be. The real problem lies in the levels of causal explanation which the descriptions may seem to imply. In one sense Jean Monnet a quarter of a century ago, and future historians a quarter of a century hence (if that is how things finally turn out), may agree that British participation in West European unity was historically inevitable: it was in the nature of things, it was predestined by geography, or it was the result of ineluctable global forces of population and technological (and hence political) evolution. President de Gaulle's vetoes were nothing but a temporary delaying factor, and once 1968 had undermined his power base the rest naturally followed. Approaching the picture a little more closely, others might say it all depended on Georges Pompidou. If he said 'no', no it would be, whatever all the busy Brussels bureaucrats might put in their interminable papers, and even Edward Heath could not have changed his mind. If he said 'yes' – to quote one of my friendliest and fiercest critics – 'Soames' chauffeur could have done the rest'. Yet when and why he said yes, only Pompidou's psycho-analyst could tell us (if, incongruously, he consulted one) and most probably not even he. Similarly – in domestic affairs – at one level, provided the British government decided, Parliament and people were bound to follow – so only Edward Heath mattered. At another level of explanation, personal relationships going back to student days, the generosity of a rich backer for a movement, a round of drinks in a politician's home after the formal meetings were over, a flash of inspiration to a civil servant on a technical solution, or the contingency planning which a party manager made in his bath-tub one Sunday morning (to quote actual examples given to me) were all significant factors *sine qua* perhaps *non*. A great many horses had to be shoed, and in the end none of the nails that did get lost lost the battle. Indeed one senior negotiator very seriously attributes the success of the negotiations to that least explicable of causal forces – luck.

We are thus dealing with factors that range from secular world trends to those of the order of Cleopatra's nose. All one can say is that there are thousands of people whose political activities are motivated by the belief that the long-term global forces all point the opposite way, and will prove British signature of the Rome Treaty to have been a reactionary aberration. Others are by no means convinced that history did (or in the future will) take the course it ought inevitably to take, but believe it needed their personal efforts not just to hasten its timing and shape its modalities, but for 'good' to triumph over 'evil' as they see it, with no divine predestination to take their individual responsibility from their shoulders. For those who have faith in historic inevitability, I have sought to trace at any rate the how and the when. Personally I must confess to feeling that too much has happened in the world that was pointless and even 'inconceivable', that too much of what was imperative and 'inevitable' has failed to materialize, not to believe that even the 'predestined' needs a possible time and a possible way for human agents to bring it about.

What I would, however, more and more doubt is that there can, by the nature of this story, be any single 'inside' version of it. There may be an 'inside' version from the point of view of the European Move-ment, from that of Britain's Paris embassy, or from that of the Com-mission's negotiating task-force; there may be one from the point of view of the Labour Marketeers, from that of Keep Britain Out, or from that of the Independent Television News. But each of these is a different story. Any attempt at putting them all in a common perspective must remain a subjective exercise, and therefore any 'definitive' version of 'how things actually happened' is in principle inconceivable. Not only do we have to weave about between layers on the onion. In the end, the onion has no heart.

Whereof one cannot speak, thereof must one be silent? I think not.

For a book of this kind is concerned not simply with the elusive heart of the onion, but with the search for it and with the intrinsic character of its different parts in their different layers. The purpose of telling the story – and telling it at particular different levels in different parts – is not simply to explain how Britain acceded to the Rome Treaty. This chronicle is concerned just as much or more with an attempt to explain how in one instance the process of decision actually worked. It is meant, in other words, as a quarry not simply for the historian, but also for the political scientist, or (to use a more modest description) the student of politics as a system of regulating society.

Certainly, agreed, the instance here described is atypical in two respects. For one thing, within Britain it cut right across the established party lines. Whether the demands of modern social problems will produce an increasing number of such cross-party divisions it is too early to say with certitude, but there are signs that this will not be an isolated instance. Moreover, both in the diplomatic and in the domestic aspects of the story we are dealing with a complex case that does not fall into any single text-book category. But it is a type of decision-making into which we are more and more being pushed by events, whether we like it or not. Decisions have more and more to be taken and implemented in multiple dimensions: in different countries simultaneously; in national, international and 'supranational' spheres; by a degree of concurrence between politicians, diplomats, civil servants, economic power-holders, opinion-formers, and various elements of the public; and on matters that transcend the frontiers of law and economics, of social and political life. In that sense, though historic truth is impossible, and obviously the task needed far more time, for me not to publish now would have been to commit *la trahison des clercs*.

Standlake Manor, Oxfordshire
September 1972

Introduction: Time-Lags in Political Psychology

There is one thing you British will never understand: an idea. And there is one thing you are supremely good at grasping: a hard fact. We will have to build Europe without you: but then you will come in and join us

Jean Monnet

This book focuses on the years 1970–72, when the government of Britain negotiated her accession to the three European Communities, and Parliament made that accession legally possible. The present Introduction, therefore, briefly sketches the reasons why the six Continental countries formed their Communities in the first place, and why Britain stood aside at that time. The answer to the first question must be sought largely in the years leading up to the Schuman Plan of 1950. The answer to the second differed in two successive phases – the decade of the 'fifties when Britain, though urgently pressed to join, refused to do so, and that of the 'sixties when successive British governments, now anxious to join, were prevented from doing so.[1] Only in 1971 did the will and the power appear at last to coincide for Britain: and even then the contemporary chronicler cannot take it for granted that the conclusion of the constitutional process entails the final settlement of the political issue.

The Mainsprings of the European Movement, 1945–50

The political impetus for the unification of Europe effectively dates from the closing stages of the Second World War. Those were the years when leading statesmen all over the world, following the principles laid down in the Allies' war aims, sought to create a far stronger League of Nations, a United Nations, even a federation of the world. Shocked by the legal and illegal crimes against humanity which they had witnessed in the previous decade, both in the pre-war dictatorships and during the war itself, appalled by the vast problems of hunger and want facing every part of the world at the end of that conflict, the

[1] In retelling this story I have naturally drawn on my earlier accounts of the same periods, notably in *The Challenge of the Common Market*, Blackwell, Oxford, 1961, and in the Introduction to A. Moncrieff (ed.), *Britain and the Common Market 1967*, BBC, London, 1967.

World Federalist movement took as its main aim the abolition of physical force as a method of diplomacy, the abatement or abolition of national sovereignty, and the creation of a body of international law in the full sense of the term, pronounced and sanctioned by a world authority.

The San Francisco Conference of 1944 did not fulfil these hopes. It produced a United Nations which has certainly shown itself stronger than the old League, but is still not even a confederation of states, let alone a world government. Its General Assembly remains an assembly of governments exercising their sovereignty – not one of representatives of the people deliberating in common for the common good. The final contradiction of these dreams of the war years was to be found in the national right of disobedience to any UN majority decision, formally recognized by the right of veto given to the five nations then regarded as big. So hopes for a world government were dashed to the ground.

By 1947 it was clear that more intensive international co-operation was possible only on a less extensive front. A tighter bond could be forged only between a smaller number of nations. Failing progress on a world scale, the countries of Europe (for which the federalists in Europe felt they had the most immediate responsibility) were to set an example to the world. For some idealists at least, European unity was thus not simply a regionalist approach for its own sake but a pilot project for something to come on a wider scale: any abdication of sovereignty, even on a regional basis, seemed better than allowing the nation state to consolidate itself once more after its great moral and material bankruptcy.

It was in Britain in particular that the World Federalist strain was intertwined with the ideal of European federation. The result was not entirely happy. Since federalists were among the most active in post-war relief and in international meetings, Europeans (who could not always tell an English crank from a normal Englishman) overestimated their strength in Britain. The moral absolutism and salvationist dogma of many of the early post-war federalists stemmed from their belief that federation was a technical prerequisite for translating the Sermon on the Mount into practice in the twentieth century. But because in their preoccupation with ultimate aims many federalists seemed starry-eyed, British observers were tempted to write off the federalists on the Continent as equally cranky and unrepresentative. For a very long time British policy was affected by this image of federalists as outsiders who were not to be taken quite seriously. All the greater was

British surprise when they did succeed in pulling off some of their curious plans.

There was indeed a profound difference in outlook and psychology on the two sides of the Channel. In her finest hour Britain had stood alone. She was undefeated, she had escaped occupation, she had not known bitter internal cleavages, she had no feelings of guilt, but came through with greater self-confidence, greater pride in her national virtues and national institutions, than she had known for years. The Continent, on the other hand, had just passed through the worst ordeal of its history. Almost every family had experienced the effects of nationalism run riot, almost every country had been subjected first to national defeat and then to enemy occupation. Their national self-confidence, their national institutions had been shattered. Starting from the ruins, it was imperative to develop new conceptions and more radical ideas that would make any future civil war between European brother nations impossible. In Continental Europe, a federal surrender of sovereignty thus seemed more feasible than in many as yet less disillusioned parts of the globe.

Common opposition to the Hitler regime had brought Resistance fighters and exile governments of different nationalities closer together: against Hitler's new order for a united Europe under Nazi domination, the men from the *maquis* and other underground movements set an alternative ideal. As activists of nine European Resistance movements expressed it in July 1944: 'Federal Union alone can ensure the preservation of liberty and civilization on the Continent of Europe, bring about economic recovery, and enable the German people to play a peaceful role in European affairs.'[1] For, if common fear of a third wave of German aggression seemed a bond that could unite many nations for some time, the more far-sighted also knew that it would be impossible to discriminate against Germany for ever. Any such attempt would fail and breed just what it was designed to prevent. If German policy was to be subjected to international controls, and if Germany was to be an equal member in the European family of nations, then there was only one way out of the dilemma – other nations must abdicate to supra-national bodies the same measure of sovereignty which they intended Germany never to regain.

Winston Churchill, then Leader of the British Opposition, saw much

[1] 'Draft Declaration by the European Resistance Movements, July 1944', reprinted in Kitzinger, *The European Common Market and Community*, Routledge, London, 1967, pp. 29–33.

the same problem: in Zurich in 1946, he called for European unity to be based on 'something that will astonish you . . . a partnership between France and Germany'. But Britain was not included in this concept of 'a kind of United States of Europe' which Churchill advocated: 'France and Germany must take the lead together. Great Britain . . . America, and I trust Soviet Russia . . . must be the friends and sponsors of the new Europe'[1] – its friends, but not part of it. Indeed the notion of a partnership with Germany proved a far more unpopular one for far longer in Britain than it did in Belgium, Holland or France, who were closer to Germany geographically, had been under occupation, in some ways had had to differentiate between Germans on other than purely national criteria, and wanted more quickly to forget experiences which were not always of their proudest. In Britain, on the other hand, emotions about Germans as such had remained less challenged by concrete experience, and were cherished by a whole generation – all the more so as the country increasingly found herself almost needing the memory of a dragon to recall her heroic role as St George. Not perhaps till the emotionalism had – temporarily – swung almost too far in the other direction at the time of the Queen's visit to Germany in 1965 did this mistrust from the past cease to be an appreciable factor in British attitudes towards building a joint future together with Germany and France.

World federalism in general, and the specific European problem of Germany, thus formed the first two mainsprings of West European integration. Soon, however, the memories of the last enemy became less real than the fear of a new aggressor. Armed Soviet Communism had advanced to the Elbe and beyond, and French and Italian Communism was showing its strength in parliamentary and direct action as far as the Channel and the Pyrenees. The year 1948 saw the Communist *coup* in Prague and the beginning of the Berlin blockade. In the face of this immediate common threat of terrifying proportions, national differences loomed less large, and some important Continental countries hoped to shore up the instabilities in their own political systems by being contained in a broader-based framework. Common defence, a common front in foreign policy, and political solidarity at home seemed the only way for non-Communist Europe to survive the new pressures applied to it from within as well as without.

Here, too, things looked rather different from the other side of the Channel. There was no domestic Communist menace worth mention

[1] For the bulk of the text of this speech see Kitzinger, op. cit., pp. 33–7.

either under the Labour government of 1945-51 or thereafter. And the external menace was not one of being overrun in a matter of hours by Soviet land troops, but of air and, in due course, nuclear strikes and longer-term pressures. It was hardly surprising if, given a lesser menace and one which took a somewhat different form, Britain chose, instead of integrating politically with the exposed countries to the south and east of her, to remain turned westwards whence her salvation had come in the two World Wars, and where by the 'forties and early 'fifties the only credible counterpoise and deterrent to Soviet conventional forces were to be found. It was in the special relationship with the United States that she sought protection and a certain guiding influence on the evolution of the balance of world power.

Fourthly, a number of the Continental countries were troubled over the relative position of Europe in the world, not simply *vis-à-vis* Russia (and the United States), but also with regard to the rest of the globe. The rise of the countries of Asia and Africa to a new influence and a new power in world affairs occupied much of federalist thought. Their idealization of European tradition forced some of the older European federalists of the time to take a gloomy view of mankind's prospects in this imminent shift in the configuration of world power. European political unity would not stem the tide. But some (particularly French) circles hoped it would at least buttress the 'civilizing presence' of Europe overseas, while others, faced with the same situation at one remove, felt unity was desperately needed to rehabilitate Europe morally in the eyes of world opinion, and to mark the abandonment of the national concept by the very nations that had served as the model for nationalism overseas. Given the rate of expansion of the Afro-Asian countries, economic unity might produce a margin of economic manœuvre that would allow Europe to provide more aid to those countries and thereby cushion and guide, even as it accelerated, their progress to positions of world power.

Here, too, things looked very different from Westminster. The contrast for Britain seemed not to be between national policies and European ones, but between Europe and the Commonwealth. Both to the Labour government, which saw the multi-racial Commonwealth as a potential world-wide bridge between the rich and the poor, the black, the brown and the white, and to Conservatives, who valued it in terms of the proven loyalty of the white Dominions in two World Wars, Europe could be at most a complement, but never a rival to the Commonwealth concept. Britain, as Winston Churchill put it in

1950, stood at the intersection of three overlapping circles – the English-speaking world, the Commonwealth, and Europe. It was by her unique position within all three that she would still, even after the Second World War, have an opportunity of playing a unique world role. Therefore none of these three bonds, and certainly not that with Europe, could afford to be tightened to the extent that they might damage the other two.

To support the common defence effort, the common political influence, and the joint positive enterprises within Europe for the future, it seemed essential on the Continent to reconstruct the devastated national economies, not separately, but by co-operation: only common efforts could make the best use of the scant resources available. Thus on the Continent economic unity was advocated by free-trade liberals who wished to diminish the restrictive effects of political boundaries and the influence of national governments on economic life. Yet among its foremost champions there were also those who regarded the national economy as too small an entity for effective planning, and who strove to set up supranational authorities to direct production and trade on a vaster international scale.

On the Continent the European Movement thus cut right across the domestic political disputes in economic affairs. In Britain the same was true, but in the opposite sense. In the late 'forties and early 'fifties British standards of living, British income per head, and the strength of the British economy had seemed – indeed, at that time were – greatly superior to those of most of the Continent (see page 29 for the 1950 figures). While Britain was prepared to make some sacrifices in the immediate post-war period (introducing bread rationing after the war to help feed defeated enemies), there seemed little to be gained from economic integration with nations suffering from such economic difficulties – quite apart from their social problems and their political instability. The Labour government up to 1951 wanted to set up a welfare state, if not actual Socialism, in one country; after 1951 the Conservative government wanted to 'set the people free'. Neither party wanted to load itself with the burden of open-ended economic commitments to the Continent and of compromising their own economic policy with the ideas of the Continentals – interpreted by one side as high capitalism, by the other as dirigist planning. So on this fifth count, too, the same type of reasoning which on the Continent had led to the conclusion that Western Europe must integrate, on the other side of the Channel also led to the corollary that Britain must keep

away from any supranational integration that involved a formal surrender of sovereignty, and go no further than co-operation between
national governments – at least unless the United States was equally
involved.

It was here that the 'functionalists' (to use the phraseology of the
period), who were most strongly represented by the British and
Scandinavian governments, parted company with the 'federalists', who
were well represented in the governments of France, Italy and the
Low Countries. It was the hallmark of the 'federalist' that he sought
joint action not least as a means for obtaining more effective common
political institutions, whereas the 'functionalist' attempted to set up
only that minimum of political institutions that was indispensable in
order to direct the common action that was most urgently required.
While the federalist may be accused of concentrating excessively on
legal formalities, the functionalist may have underrated the handicap
imposed on effective everyday co-operation by the survival of national
vetoes. Federalists and functionalists in the late 'forties failed fully to
understand each other, and the federalists – not by accident, but for
good historical reasons – were able to sway the policy of six and only
six of the countries of Western Europe. What they achieved was
something less than a United States of Europe, though Jean Monnet's
Action Committee for a United States of Europe retained a more
maximalist title. Yet though the terminology, the fervour and the
time-scale of objectives changed with the passage of time, this
original contrast and even conflict between federalists and functionalists
was to mark the whole history of post-war Europe.

But there were divergencies even within the federalist camp. The
United States' insistence on European co-operation had been one of
the conditions of Marshall Aid. The United States was welcomed as
an ally by most of those who sought to unite Europe; yet they were far
from agreeing on the policy which Europe was to pursue towards the
United States once it had been united. The campaign for European
unity as such was thus, in fact, neutral between two sets of corre-
lative political and economic concepts. Political unity was advocated as
tending to enhance European freedom of movement – whether towards a more equal partnership within a strong Atlantic alliance or
towards a more independent position in the world as a third force.
Whichever way that decision might go, only unity, it was argued,
could make it effective.

There was a parallel ambivalence or mixture of economic aims.

Economic unity, with its advantages of larger markets and greater specialization of production, was advocated as a means of redressing the balance of dollar payments. But for some the first objective was to form a regional bloc embracing only Europe and the countries associated with it overseas, while others saw the discriminatory removal of economic barriers (between the countries of Europe, but not yet against the rest of the world) as a tactical move to strengthen the economies of Europe for full convertibility and non-discriminatory trading relationships with the world as a whole.

Even the historic cleavage of clericals and anticlericals was bridged by the European idea. Certainly three of the men in the van of the movement were devout Catholics born in Lothair's middle kingdom, an area where the liberal conception of the world and its denizens as naturally divisible into neat nation states appears unsophisticated in the extreme: Robert Schuman, a German during the First World War and then Prime Minister of France; Alcide de Gasperi, a Deputy in the Vienna Diet while Austria-Hungary was at war with Italy, and then Prime Minister of Italy; and Konrad Adenauer, the non-combatant anti-Prussian mayor of Cologne who flirted with the idea of separating the Rhineland from Prussia after the First World War. To them, the restoration of Charlemagne's empire of a thousand years before, with the cultural unity it implied, had an emotional appeal. But the stalwarts of the movement came also from the ranks of the anticlerical Left, organized, in the early post-war years, in the Socialist Movement for a United States of Europe. The Socialist Paul-Henri Spaak, a former Belgian Prime Minister, provided the personal driving force in the drafting of the Rome Treaties, and the French Socialist leader Guy Mollet was Prime Minister during the critical phases of the Common Market negotiations and secured the votes of 100 out of the 101 French Socialist deputies in favour of their ratification.

The European idea was thus originally neutral in foreign policy between a third-force concept and the Atlantic Alliance, undecided in trade policy between regionalism and multilateralism, ambivalent in its attitude to the problems of emergent nations in Africa and Asia, silent in cultural and educational matters between Catholicism and anticlericalism, and neutral also in economic policy between *laissez-faire* liberalism and Socialist planning. Approached from very diverse points of view, European unity seemed to make sense to Continental leaders, to small but highly articulate pressure groups, and to many of the war and post-war generation. It would give greater scope to Europe for whatever policy aims were envisaged. A sudden realization of Continental federation could have produced sharp conflicts over the use to which unity was to be put; as it was, the long common struggle and the course of post-war events softened the contrasts of ultimate aim and produced not merely international but also inter-party understanding. Only the Communists in every parliament of the Six consistently voted against integration.

Britain and the Communities, 1950–70

The story has often been told of how, in 1950, six countries and six only sought to advance beyond the looser and wider organizations of NATO, the Organization for European Economic Co-operation, and the Council of Europe (in all of which Britain was a member). They set up their Coal and Steel Community as a first step to a general common market and economic community, and they worked out detailed blueprints for a defence community, and for a political community to overarch the rest. Though they failed with the last two, they then succeeded with the EEC and Euratom. Britain's various attempts – through Western European Union, through the Free Trade Area proposals, and by various other arrangements – to get the best of both worlds, as both 'in' and yet not 'of' the emergent Europe, are equally familiar. What is relevant to the theme of this book are the reasons for which, by 1961, the British government had completely changed tack and made its application for negotiations to see if terms could be found on which she could, after all, join the endeavours she had cold-shouldered only five years before.

There were five milestones on that road to Damascus. The first came as early as 1956 with the Suez disaster: even in a traditional sphere of influence, even acting together with an ally, nineteenth-century gunboat tactics had proved humiliatingly self-defeating, and thus the first crack appeared in British post-war self-confidence. With angry young men challenging social smugness and the Campaign for Nuclear Disarmament challenging Britain's image of her place in the world (let alone the forms which military power was assuming in that world), self-questioning became a little more widespread.

Then came the fateful year of 1960, in which the abandonment of Blue Streak on technical and financial grounds represented the abandonment of Britain's claim to any truly independent military deterrent; the collapse of the Paris summit meeting, the last occasion on which a British Prime Minister attempted to play a major role at the top table of world diplomacy; and the first of that series of sterling crises which was to dog the British economy right through the 'sixties, though successive governments of both political parties sacrificed domestic economic growth to the maintenance of the dollar-sterling rate of exchange. Fifthly, there was the demand for faster economic growth at home. Performance indicators on the Continent appeared to be startlingly superior (see the table on p. 29, which shows the comparative dynamism of the Six in almost every one of its sections). Though the Labour Party had in 1959 drawn attention to the 'growth league tables' in which the British economy was shown to have performed substantially worse than most of those on the Continent, the Conservative government had shrugged them off with the slogan 'You've never had it so good'; it was only in 1960–61 that the government began to ponder seriously the slow rate of growth in Britain's national product, and turned simultaneously to a form of indicative planning modelled on the French and to the concept of a 'bracing cold shower' of competition through entry into the EEC.

It was much at the same time that there spread among policy-makers in Britain a certain scepticism as to the future of those two other overlapping circles, the Anglo-American special relationship that had been the hub of Churchill's 'English-speaking world', and the Commonwealth. In the 'fifties the Commonwealth had still looked like giving Britain increased economic scope and additional leverage in the world. In the 'sixties it became obvious that the overseas sterling area was the most stagnant sector of British exports (its share of total British exports diminished from 48% in 1950 to 30% in 1960 and then 27% in 1970) and that, so far from increasing Britain's political freedom of action, the Commonwealth tended if anything to restrict it. The notion that the Commonwealth would somehow be a means of exporting the Westminster model of parliamentary democracy and adding to the peace of the world by the sort of internal regimes it would propagate had long been abandoned in the face of experience in Africa. By the 1971 Singapore conference of Commonwealth Prime Ministers many felt that Britain almost needed liberating from a grouping that stood her in the dock and judged her according to some superior moral standard over Rhodesia – the judges being people whose own racial policies (whether in Biafra, over East African Asians, or, not much later, in Bangla Desh) were far more lacking in liberalism and human brotherhood than Britain's own. There remained a general argument about helping the underdeveloped world – a criterion of useful world citizen-

		UK	The Six	USA
Population (millions)	1950	50	157	152
	1958	52	165	174
	1970	56	190	205
Gross national product	1950	47	75	318
($ billion)	1958	65	163	455
	1970	121	485	993
GNP per head ($)	1950	940	477	2040
	1958	1258	955	2613
	1970	2170	2557	4760
Industrial production				
(1953=100)	1950	94	80	82
(1953=100)	1958	114	144	102
(1958=100)	1963	119	142	135
(1963=100)	1970	125	151	135
Gross fixed asset formation	1958	15·1	20·4	16·9
(% of GNP)	1970	18·0	25·0	17·0
Imports	1950	7·2	11·2	8·7
($ billion)	1958	10·5	22·9	13·3
	1970	21·7	88·4	40·0
Exports	1950	6·3	9·4	10·1
($ billion)	1958	9·3	22·8	17·9
	1970	19·4	88·5	43·2
Exports to (other) EEC	1950	0·8	3·0	1·6
countries	1958	1·3	6·9	2·4
($ billion)	1970	4·2	43·3	8·4
Official reserve assets	1950	3·4	2·9	22·8
($ billion)	1958	3·1	11·8	20·6
	1970	2·8	29·8	14·5
Development aid				
(net official flow $ billion)	1958	0·3	1·3	2·4
	1970	0·4	2·1	3·1

Sources: United Nations Statistical Year Books, OEEC and OECD monthly
Statistics, and Development Assistance Committee annual reports.

ship in which the Six could claim a recent record by no means inferior to Britain's; there remained also one or two specific economic problems arising out of the Commonwealth sugar agreement or the New Zealand butter trade; but the Commonwealth as an alternative power configuration had virtually disappeared from British policy-makers' minds.

Much the same was true from the early 'sixties as far as the 'special relationship' was concerned. There could be little doubt that, whatever had been true under Dwight Eisenhower's presidency, under the Kennedy administration the relationship between Washington and Bonn was coming to be in some ways at least as 'special' as that between Washington and London. The Kennedy 'grand design' of Atlantic partnership quite explicitly involved a relationship between a United States of America on one side of the Atlantic, and a fast unifying single economic and power complex on the other. Though some were surprised when it became even more obvious in late 1962, the failure of Skybolt was for President Kennedy 'the grand opportunity to terminate the special relationship and force Britain into Europe'.[1] Yet it was largely by reference to that special relationship that President de Gaulle, in early 1963, vetoed Britain's application.

Whatever the realism of looking upon the European Community as a replacement of the other two 'circles' or as a new lever for British political influence, by the end of the 'sixties the arguments had changed. The possibility that the United States might withdraw from Western Europe – a realization of the old slogan of 'US go home' – raised fears of a void in West European security which only much closer military and logistic collaboration between West European nations could convincingly fill. The spectre of 'collusion' between the United States and the Soviet Union, both of them more concerned with the pressure of China than with the dangers they once seemed to spell for each other, became an argument for diplomatic and political collaboration between Europeans anxious not to have their fate settled over their heads.

In international economics, there was a triple concern: over the comparative lack of autochthonous European technology to set against the USA's lead in research and development; over the 'American challenge' of multi-national but basically American-dominated companies spreading over Europe while remaining largely free of any

---

[1] Arthur M. Schlesinger, Jr, *A Thousand Days. John F. Kennedy in the White House*, Deutsch, London, 1965, p. 734.

effective political supervision and control; and finally over the world's monetary problems, exacerbated by the mass of footloose and uncontrolled 'Eurodollars' and the weakness of the United States balance of payments, which threatened to thrust monetary responsibilities on the Community long before it was really equipped to face them.

On Western Europe's internal problems, too, the arguments began to change once more at the very beginning of the 'seventies. In the late 'fifties and early 'sixties, economic growth as reflected in gross national product statistics had been regarded as a cardinal indicator of success; now economic growth (compounded by population increase) was continuing at such a rate that it began on the one hand to be seen more for what it is – a prerequisite for achieving social objectives which have to be politically defined – and on the other hand to be viewed with suspicion for its environmental, social and psychological costs which could not be measured in the economic dimension alone. There might be little hope that the problems of inflation (rampant at different rates in different countries) could be greatly eased at any early stage by Community action. But over as vital a problem as environmental deterioration the Community, it was argued, could act far more effect- tively than nation states on their own (with the Common Agricultural Policy one possible ingredient in its action). If the original inspiration was the fear that Western Europe might be crushed with a bang, new tasks were now discovered in preventing it from stifling itself with a whimper.

Similarly, within Britain, the argument had also changed. Where in the early 'sixties the Community was still largely a thing of hope and aspiration to be shaped by its participants, with each member and possible member reading into its potential those policies which corres- ponded to his own needs, by now detailed policies had taken shape on barley prices and on value added tax, on lorry-axle pressure and on food additives. Tailored to suit the six member states, yet for obvious political reasons impossible to nullify and rejig all over again, these policies could not be expected to be optimal for late entrants who had refused to join at the beginning. The combination of an agricultural policy and a fiscal system which taxed imports from outside the Community (on which Britain had hitherto been heavily dependent) for the benefit of farmers (of whom Britain had relatively few) would put a substantial tax burden on Britain; and the combination of high food prices and a value added tax less selective than British consumer taxation was liable to result, unless offset in other ways, in a less progressive tax system within Britain. The consequent additional obstacles to economic growth and difficulties for social policy were potent arguments against entry, at least in the short term.

At the same time, particularly in 1972, the constitutional problems were very clearly displayed. The British Parliament had to take over lock, stock and barrel forty-two volumes of legislation passed by Community institutions – whose legitimacy as democratic representatives (even of the citizens of the original Community) seemed obscure. Worse still, Parliament entered into an open-ended commitment to incorporate into British law all future Community legislation and make it virtually unamendable by the domestic Parliament. The democratic legitimacy of Community institutions may or may not be a problem that can be solved once Britain is inside the Communities. The relegation of the Westminster Parliament in matters where the Community has competence was not so much an unfortunate accidental disadvantage as inherent in the essence of the Community as such, and thus part and parcel of the aim of entry.

We thus touch on the core problem of Community-building: how far the larger unit with which men identified in politically relevant ways remained overwhelmingly the nation state, and how far both smaller subnational and wider supranational units became co-ordinate frames of reference: how far in particular the political use of the word 'we' referred to West Europeans rather than to the British people.

Nothing perhaps illustrates more convincingly the difference between the British public and the population of the Six in their identification with a wider than national group, and their view of the need for wider institutions to take decisions for that group, than the opinion polls commissioned simultaneously in seven countries in early 1970 by the EEC itself. (Their results are set out on page 33.) Whereas on the Continent every single question elicited a clear preponderance of 'Europeans', in Britain the 'Europeans' remained on every single question in a minority. While Continental political leaders could thus count on a fair degree of popular support for their attempts at further integration, the lag between the British public and the Continental public, the British public and the British political leadership, posed serious problems of domestic persuasion, and no doubt also helped make more difficult the problems of foreign diplomacy.

There thus remained profound differences: differences of attitude between the Continent and Britain; acute conflicts in Britain between long-run and short-run, political and economic objectives; divergencies

A Comparative Poll in Seven Countries

Are you in favour of, or against, Britain joining the European Common Market?

	Holland	Luxem-burg	West Germany	France	Belgium	Italy	EEC	Britain
In favour	79	70	69	66	63	51	64	19
Against	8	6	7	11	8	9	8	63
Don't know	13	24	24	23	29	40	28	18

Assuming that Britain did join, would you be for or against the evolution of the Common Market towards the political formation of a United States of Europe?

	Holland	Luxem-burg	West Germany	France	Belgium	Italy	EEC	Britain
For	64	75	69	67	60	60	65	30
Against	17	5	9	11	10	7	9	48
Don't know	19	20	22	22	30	33	26	22

Would you be in favour of, or against the election of a European parliament by direct universal suffrage; that is a parliament elected by all the voters in the member countries?

	Holland	Luxem-burg	West Germany	France	Belgium	Italy	EEC	Britain
In favour	59	71	66	59	56	55	59	25
Against	21	10	9	15	11	6	11	55
Don't know	20	19	25	26	33	39	30	20

Would you be willing to accept, over and above your own government, a European Government responsible for a common policy in foreign affairs, defence and the economy?

	Holland	Luxem-burg	West Germany	France	Belgium	Italy	EEC	Britain
Willing	50	47	57	49	51	51	53	22
Not willing	32	35	19	28	19	10	20	60
Don't know	18	18	24	23	30	39	27	18

If a President of a United States of Europe were being elected by popular vote, would you be willing to vote for a candidate not of your own country – if his personality and programme corresponded more closely to your ideas than those of the candidates of your own country?

	Holland	Luxem-burg	West Germany	France	Belgium	Italy	EEC	Britain
Willing	63	67	69	61	52	45	59	39
Not willing	18	20	20	22	24	19	18	41
Don't know	19	13	19	17	24	36	23	20

of tactics between British policy-makers; and not least a gulf between policy-makers and people. It is really with the attempts to bridge all these gaps more or less at one and the same time that this book is concerned. Its first part is devoted to the problems of diplomacy posed for the government abroad; its second to the tasks of persuading the public at home of what the policy-makers had decided was the best road for the country to take.

PART ONE

1 The General Begins to Shift?

La guerre des guerres, le combat des combats, c'est de l'Angleterre et de la France; le reste est episode

Jules Michelet

Rival Theories

On 27 November 1967, Charles de Gaulle, in an almost boisterous press conference, vetoed British entry for the second time. Less than three and a half years later, on 21 May 1971, his successor, Georges Pompidou, all smiles at an Elysée banquet, spoke of 'two peoples . . . trying to find each other again to take part in a great joint endeavour' and claimed a 'complete identity of view on the working and development of the Community'. President Pompidou himself recognized the paradox, the total reversal of policy, in his opening sentence affirming 'friendship and warmth': 'What could be more normal? And yet, today, what could be more spectacular?'

Here in Paris, far more than anywhere else, lay the crux of the issue whether Britain's accession to the EEC would or would not be possible. Had French foreign policy on the issue really veered by 180 degrees? Until May 1971 this remained the riddle of the Sphinx. So the question of just what happened, when, and why, to eliminate France's veto is the most central problem in explaining the difference between failure in 1963, failure in 1967 – and finally success in 1971.

The trail for an explanation naturally leads to Paris. And in Paris responsible senior officials close to the personalities and events of our story give totally contradictory answers as to both the timing and the motivation of the process. What is certain is that – as in the case of the Labour Party in Britain – answers as to the past are inevitably influenced by attitudes in the present: as always, history serves as a political weapon for ongoing battles and to prepare positions for the future.

Let us set out the two extreme theories to be heard on the other side of the Channel. Obviously there is a whole gamut of alternative explanations on the (not entirely one-dimensional) scale between them. But the two extremes will serve to define the area within which we must look for the most likely story.

On the one side is what one might call the 'hard' theory. The decision to allow Britain in was not taken until spring 1971, after genuine attempts by the French to resist the British initiative. It was only taken when there was no longer any viable alternative: when the pressure of the 'other five', culminating in blackmail from Willy Brandt and Emilio Colombo, forced Pompidou to give way. Germany and Italy threatened retaliation bordering on the break-up of the EEC; but the Community had become vital to France, and her national interests would have been hurt more by keeping Britain out than by letting her in. Only then did Pompidou, like a good diplomat, suddenly consent to see Heath, turn on the charm, and reap what credit he could both from the other five and from the applicant nations.

At the opposite end of the scale is the 'soft' theory. President de Gaulle started it all himself, and Pompidou was only continuing along the course which his illustrious predecessor had himself begun to steer. Had not de Gaulle, on 4 February 1969, received Christopher Soames and spoken to him honeyed words designed as a first step towards drawing Britain into the construction of a political Europe after all? If, when the British behaved so intolerably afterwards, nothing more came of it in the remaining weeks of de Gaulle's tenure of office, that was hardly his fault. Pompidou asserted at his very first presidential press conference in July 1969 that there was no objection of principle to British entry, and if it still took another two years to consummate that policy – well, major changes cannot be achieved in a hurry.

Clearly there are psychological and political advantages for different sets of people in each of these lines of explanation. The Quai d'Orsay worked hard on a tough negotiation (which might have made the British Prime Minister give up in despair of ever obtaining terms that could get through the House of Commons). Naturally they may not want to believe afterwards that they were expendable pawns pushed forward by a political master who intended to let the British through in any case, and to make them look ridiculous in having to reverse their negotiating positions overnight later on. It is not surprising that they should give Pompidou credit for having been faithful for as long as he could to the consistent French position that they fought to defend right through the 'sixties. Conversely it must suit the book of the Gaullist

party managers to represent Pompidou as faithful throughout, and
even now, to the General: and to argue that it was de Gaulle who had
already come to the conclusion that Britain either could not be kept
out or else positively ought at some stage to be brought in – in other
words, that the vital decisions had already been taken or prepared as
early as the winter of 1968–69.

There is no alternative to going over the period between the two
dates with both these theories in mind, looking for clues.

The General's Vetoes

President de Gaulle's public reasoning on 27 November 1967 differed
slightly from that of 14 January 1963, the time of the first veto.[1] The
emphasis in 1963 was on Britain's overseas relationships: 'England is,
in effect, insular, maritime, linked through its trade, markets and food
supply to very diverse and often very distant countries.' He stressed the
fear that if Britain (and, in her train, other European countries)
entered the Community 'in the end there would appear a colossal
Atlantic Community under American dependence and leadership
which would soon completely swallow up the European Community'. De Gaulle went on to discuss Nassau, rejecting the offer of
Polaris missiles and noting in passing that, in the building of submarines
and warheads, the British had received privileged assistance from the
Americans which had never been offered to – or asked for by – France.
He then invited a question on Germany to stress that France and
Germany 'in thought, philosophy, science, the arts and technology are
complementary' and declared himself 'overwhelmed by the elemental
and extraordinary outbursts of enthusiasm displayed in favour of the
friendship of Germany and France, of the union of Europe as they both
wish it and of their common action in the world' and 'touched to the
very depths of my soul and strengthened in my conviction that the new
policy of Franco–German relations rests on incomparable popular
support' It was basically a contrast of Anglo-Saxons against Continentals, free traders against builders of a tight community, a choice
in favour of Germany as against the Americans' Trojan horse.

[1] For the relevant passages from the two press conferences see Kitzinger, op. cit.,
pp. 182–94 and Kitzinger, *The Second Try*, Pergamon Press, Oxford, 1968,
pp. 311–17. The November 1967 press conference had been preceded by the
'velvet veto' of the 16 May 1967 press conference, large parts of which are
reprinted in Harold Wilson, *The Labour Government 1964–70: A Personal Record*,
Weidenfeld and Nicolson and Michael Joseph, London, 1971, pp. 392–4.

In the November 1967 press conference, after harking back to Britain's earlier opposition to the EEC, he declared what was needed was 'a radical transformation of Great Britain, to enable her to join the Continentals. This is obvious from the political point of view.' But in his detailed argument he concentrated on economics, and particularly on monetary affairs:

The Common Market is incompatible with Great Britain's economy as it stands, in which the chronic balance of payments deficit is proof of its permanent imbalance and which, as concerns production, sources of supply, credit practices and working conditions, involves factors which that country could not alter without modifying its own nature. . . .

The Common Market is further incompatible with the restrictions imposed by Great Britain on exports of capital which, on the contrary, circulates freely among the Six.

The Common Market is incompatible with the state of sterling, as once again highlighted by the devaluation, together with the loans that have preceded and are accompanying it; also the state of sterling which, combined with the pound's character as an international currency and the enormous external debts weighing on it, would not allow the country to be part of the solid, interdependent and assured society in which the Franc, the Mark, the Lira, the Belgian Franc and the Florin are brought together.

Under these conditions it would obviously mean breaking up a Community that was built and operates according to rules which do not tolerate such a monumental exception.

The public record of the time on the General's motivations can now be supplemented with the memoirs of the two British Ministers who then confronted him. Harold Wilson's story of his private meetings with de Gaulle emphasizes the General's worries concerning the effect of enlargement on the Community:

He then went on to a theme which was to become familiar during the year – the nature of the Community as it was, and was becoming, and how the entry of new countries might affect it. The Treaty was not itself a reality – it was simply a treaty – but its application had created certain realities, difficult as that application had been, both in the industrial and economic field and also – and here the difficulties had been very great indeed – in agriculture.[1]

And clearly what worried him most of all in private was still the same as in 1963 – 'the mortal sin of Atlanticism':

[1] Wilson, op. cit., pp. 334–41 and esp. 407–18.

He had always observed, in war and peace, and whether or not Britain really wanted it, that she was linked to the United States. Thus, if Britain joined in her present condition and even if the British Government did not state or think that this was their purpose, Britain would introduce an element that inclined towards an Atlantic type of Community.

Moreover, as I well knew, certain members of the Six were also favourable to it, though possibly less so than Britain. He then proceeded to list them in lofty tones, with the indication that they were only restrained from the mortal sin of Atlanticism by the firmness of the General.

'*Les Hollandais*' – they were strongly in favour of the Atlantic concept. '*Les Belges*' – more or less equally so. '*Les Allemands*' – they would be very tempted. '*Les pauvres Italiens*' – they, being directly dependent on the United States, could not hope to prevent it.[1]

George Brown, recording his solo encounter with de Gaulle late in 1966, confirms the General's attitude and demonstrates that the Labour government had no evidence of any change in it. But he also adds the General's preoccupation with the EEC's internal balance:

It was very clear that de Gaulle was adamantly against us. He regarded the Continent as France's place and the Atlantic Ocean and the United States as Britain's place. It was at this meeting that de Gaulle made his famous remark about the impossibility of two cocks living in one farmyard with ten hens. He said that he had had a lot of trouble getting the five hens to do what France wanted, and he wasn't going to have Britain's coming in and creating trouble all over again, this time with ten.[2]

It was no doubt in indirect reply to these kinds of thought that Harold Wilson, in the intimacy of 'a small French car, about the size of a British 1100 saloon, . . . the General, somehow, wrapping his legs into the small space available', in June 1967 tried to play the German card when the two men met at Versailles:

In international affairs, surely the one thing he had to fear was an increase in the relative strength of Germany . . . did he not fear that post-de Gaulle France, particularly if his forecast of a period of anarchy and division were realised, would be relegated to second-class status against the power of a strong Germany? . . . This surely was a case he must see for greater British involvement in the political affairs of Europe. He said he was very well aware of these questions. But he would not then have the responsibility. *Après moi* – probably what was in his mind was what he had said in the afternoon was the

[1] ibid., p. 409.
[2] George Brown, *In My Way*, Gollancz, London, 1971, p. 220.

determinant: Europe would become 'Atlantic', and while he had the power, he was not going to speed the process.

Certainly the General repeatedly assured his British interlocutors that he had understood certain changes in Britain's position. On the military side, as Wilson puts it, 'We had just decided not to ask for the Poseidon missile in place of Polaris. To that extent I was presenting him not with a new Nassau but a Nassau in reverse. Trianon was the opposite of Rambouillet,' and this was noted by the General. On the other hand in monetary matters 'he had not, he said, found me too explicit about the future role I envisaged for the pound sterling . . . our attitude and policy towards sterling still seemed to be very closely linked with United States financial policy'.[1] But then, since monetary had some time earlier come to replace military affairs as the General's chosen battlefield against the United States, the changes in Britain's defence policy were hardly as decisive in the General's eyes as some might have imagined.

These changes, which President de Gaulle recognized even in his press conferences, were insufficient: what was required was a profound economic and political transformation. What he had said in 1963 he repeated in May 1967 and then again in November: other sorts of trading arrangements might be possible with Britain, but the day for British entry into the Community had not yet come. 'If Britain one day reaches that stage, with what great joy will France then greet this historic transformation.'

So in the communiqué which in effect interred the second try, the EEC Council of Ministers noted 'that no member state raised an objection of principle against the enlargement of the Communities', but France stood out against the rest on two points: 'One state, however, expressed the opinion that this enlargement would modify profoundly the nature and the ways of administering the Communities.' And 'one member state considered that the process of restoring the British economy must be completed for Britain's application to be reconsidered'.[2] The chief overt stumbling blocks were agriculture and sterling, involving Britain's relationship with the United States on the second, and Britain's balance of payments on both the first and the second counts.

---

[1] Wilson, op. cit., pp. 413, 408, 337.
[2] Communiqué of 19 December 1967 (reprinted in *The Second Try*, ed. cit., pp. 317–18).

The Fateful Last Twelve Months

All that was in 1967. It marks the point of departure, over which there is no disagreement. The record is full, well-corroborated and unambiguous. It is only on what happened thereafter that the theories differ.

In spring 1968 de Gaulle was outwardly at his most self-willed, independent and self-confident ever. The previous year, on top of vetoing British entry, he had been active with deliberate conspicuousness in the most diverse areas. In the Middle East he had taken sides against Israel, as much perhaps in opposition to the United States as from any sympathy for Arabs in general. In North America, he had astounded the world (some claimed, actually, even himself) by his slogan of '*Vive le Québec libre*' – again as much perhaps in opposition to the Anglo-Saxons as in pursuit of linguistic and cultural Frenchdom. He had gone a long way in his monetary *politique du pire*, attacking the dollar exchange standard both directly and through 'the soft underbelly of sterling' – again combining his attack on the Anglo-Saxons with the pursuit of other objectives. Having ended most of his military participation in NATO in 1966, he was content to let speculation run as to whether he would withdraw from the alliance altogether on its twentieth anniversary in 1969, when the Treaty allowed. Early in 1968 he came out in favour of his old idea of military defence against all comers – the logical corollary of his policy of independence from the United States as much as from the Soviet Union,[1] and considered doubling or tripling his nuclear submarine programme or building his own intercontinental ballistic missiles.

This atmosphere of dramatic foreign activity on all points of the compass was accompanied by an appearance of bored quiescence at home. National product had risen, since the General came to power in 1958, by an average of 5% per annum in real terms. Wages had nearly doubled under his presidency while consumer prices had risen by less than half. Unemployment was insignificant. The gold and foreign exchange reserves had risen from $1 billion in 1958 to nearly $7 billion, equal to more than six months' imports, a ratio unparalleled even by the Germans. The French economic miracle was holding its own against the much-vaunted German performance, and *per capita* national product in France was – with the exception of tiny

[1] The doctrine was set out by Charles Ailleret, 'Défense "dirigée" ou défense "tous azimuts"', *Revue de Défense Nationale*, December 1967.

Luxemburg – the highest in the Community. What did it matter that the foundations for this expansion had been laid by the deliberate imposition of sacrifices on the voters of the Fourth Republic by its long-term planners (notably Jean Monnet and Étienne Hirsch)? The fruits in terms of consumer satisfaction were being reaped by the Gaullist regime. Election results, with the one exception of the first ballot in 1965, were satisfactory, the Parliament more or less side-tracked, the society so 'apoliticized' that no clouds on the horizon could be detected, in April 1968, by skilled political observers not a stone's throw from the Boulevard Saint-Germain where, within weeks, the stones were flying.

The events of May 1968, when a mishandled student disturbance discredited authority and triggered off strikes all over France, reducing the country to chaos for almost a fortnight, have been repeatedly analysed from diverse points of view. All that matters here are their effects on the President's stance in foreign policy in general and on Britain's role in Western Europe in particular. The possible effects were two. Directly, the political self-confidence of the General's regime was seriously undermined (in spite of the thumping electoral majority it received on 30 June 1968 in reaction against the disorders). Indirectly, de Gaulle had to count the economic cost first of the strikes and then of the wage-rises and other reforms with which discontent was bought off.

Two further developments, this time outside France, must also be cited for their possible effects on the General's thinking. On 31 March 1968 President Johnson announced not only that he would not accept another term of office, but that he had ordered an end to the bombing of most of North Vietnam, adding: 'We are prepared to move immediately towards peace through negotiations. . . . I am taking the first steps to de-escalate the conflict.' At the end of October all bombing stopped and the National Liberation Front was accepted as a partner in the peace talks. The image of a militarist, imperialist USA was beginning to look less convincing. It was not in itself, perhaps, a major factor in de Gaulle's attitude to the Anglo-Saxons, but it combined with several other twists in international relations.

For in Eastern Europe, that summer, there was a far more dramatic development; if it pointed back to the division of the world along cold-war lines, it yet had in effect parallel lessons for French policy. Czechoslovakia was invaded by Soviet tanks on the night of 20–21 August 1968. De Gaulle's first reaction was to blame it all on Yalta; as an acute observer put it: 'For the next several days the Yalta conference was the subject of nearly as much official comment and attention on the government-managed television news programmes as the invasion itself.'[1] His second reaction was to blame the West Germans for triggering off the invasion through their indiscreet 'opening to the East' – according to one eyewitness, somewhat to poor Chancellor Kurt-Georg Kiesinger's pained surprise. But what had, more seriously, become apparent was that his concept of a Europe 'from the Atlantic to the Urals' had become incompatible with his other principle of national self-determination, the principle he had been upholding in his support for Biafra and Quebec separatism. With the USA attempting to make peace in Vietnam and Brezhnev invading Czechoslovakia his policy of indifference between the blocs looked less appropriate.

So his third reaction, though he does not seem to have admitted this publicly, was his failure to withdraw from the Atlantic Alliance. By spring 1969, no doubt for a combination of financial and foreign policy reasons, General Fourquet, General Ailleret's successor, publicly rejected defence 'tous azimuts', clearly addressed himself only to 'the enemy coming from the East', and accepted the doctrine of graduated response.[2] 'Indeed', writes one authority, 'according to certain sources, Franco-American conversations on possible future collaboration in the field of nuclear weapons are said to have been started at the end of 1968.'[3]

November 1968 also witnessed the currency crisis that was largely an indirect international result of the French domestic events of the previous May. There had, of course, been a flight of suitcases full of money out of France across the borders into Belgium, Germany and Switzerland at the time of the disturbances, curbed by the introduction of severe exchange controls on 29 May. On 4 June France had to draw $745 million from the International Monetary Fund to protect the value of the franc. She did so with the blessing of the United States – a queer twist of fate, since France had twice in the preceding nine months been active in attempting to force a devaluation of the dollar. Then, to meet the bill for the 'Grenelle agreement' that had substantially settled the May strikes by raising the incomes of public employees and

[1] John Newhouse, De Gaulle and the Anglo-Saxons, Deutsch, London, 1970, p. 322.
[2] General Fourquet, Revue de Défense Nationale, May 1969. (This lecture was delivered in March 1969, well before President de Gaulle's resignation.)
[3] Guy de Carmoy, 'The Last Year of de Gaulle's Foreign Policy', International Affairs, July 1969, p. 426.

farmers, the budget had to be sharply increased. Inflation was clearly unavoidable, yet the exchange controls were rescinded on 4 September almost at the same moment as a rise in estate duties was tabled. Hundreds of millions of dollars' worth of francs again left the country in the weeks that followed to be converted – particularly into Deutschmark. The foreign exchange reserves of France fell from $6·9 billion to $4·0 billion and those of Germany rose from $8·5 billion to $10·9 billion between April and November 1968.

So on 20–22 November 1968 the Group of Ten, the inner council of the major industrial countries members of the IMF, was summoned to Bonn. Initially all the pressure was on the Germans to revalue: the Anglo-Saxons and the French – the Allies of the Second World War – were united against Germany on a major issue for the first time in many years. And, for the first time since 1945, the Germans defied them. (It is difficult for other countries to force a revaluation: reserves can always rise still higher. Forcing a devaluation is easier: reserves cannot fall below zero.) So when the Germans said 'no', the pressure was on the French. The foreign exchange markets had been closed since Wednesday, and on Friday the Group of Ten meeting dispersed having issued a communiqué that measures had been agreed to stabilize the situation: in fact, Herr Franz-Joseph Strauss was tactless enough to have himself quoted as announcing the devaluation of the French franc.

Then came the *coup de théâtre*. On Saturday the Elysée abruptly stated that the franc would not be devalued, and on Sunday de Gaulle announced stern penalties to enforce reimposed exchange restrictions, a policy of retrenchment and economies, and wage and price controls. President Johnson wired to assure de Gaulle of his support and $2 billion of credit from the Group of Ten buttressed the franc, which thus remained at its 1958 parity (thanks principally to American support) until after de Gaulle left office. The change of front forced upon the General by economic circumstances was significant. His irritation with the Germans was scarcely veiled. His dependence on the Anglo-Saxons – in whose boat he suddenly found himself with another weakened currency – was also difficult to hide.

The reconciliation with the USA was to proceed during the Nixon visit from 28 February to 2 March 1969: where all previous post-war US Presidents had assumed either that France had virtually disappeared in the war or else ought to disappear into a United Europe, Richard Nixon, fact-finding immediately after his assumption of office, found that France existed, that nation states continued to exist in Europe, that he must deal with them bilaterally, and that it was de Gaulle's leadership which had restored 'this great nation to the true place that she should hold in the family of nations'. If this is slightly to anticipate the chronology, it is only to show that by February 1969 de Gaulle's thinking on his world political strategy had changed substantially, as had his feelings on one of the two Anglo-Saxon powers whom he had in military, in monetary, in economic and in diplomatic ways been so anxious to oppose. And that may be of relevance to our interpretation of the celebrated Elysée lunch just three and a half weeks before the Nixon visit: de Gaulle's conversation with the British ambassador on 4 February 1969.

The Soames Affair

In 1968 George Brown had chosen as the new British ambassador in Paris a former Conservative front-bencher who had lost his seat in the House of Commons in 1966, Christopher Soames. It was, as indeed Brown records himself,

absolutely right. We had a lot to overcome in our relations with France. One problem was to remove a kind of arid frigidity which seemed to have settled down over all official relations between Britain and France. . . . It seemed to me that the Embassy was in all kinds of ways totally out of touch with what was really going on. . . . It needed a man with imagination, a knowledge of and a feel of France and with a particular social flair and, I am afraid, a man with some money.[1]

Soames proved a highly acceptable appointment in Paris. *Le Monde* described him at the lowest point in Franco-British relations as 'Churchill's son-in-law, who has inherited from him his very conservative views, his round shape, and his frankness. A *Croix de Guerre* won at Bir-Hakeim is witness to the long standing of his love for France.'[2]

Soames arrived in September 1968 and presented his credentials to the General, who clearly knew who he was – a politician used to taking the initiative – and what he had come for – to start up a political dialogue between the two countries. Soames set to work to convince his French friends and contacts that relations between the two countries

---

[1] Brown, op. cit., pp. 131–3. On the 'arid frigidity', however, see Lord Gore-Booth's letter in the *Sunday Times*, 1 November 1970.

[2] André Fontaine in *Le Monde*, 11 March 1969.

could hardly remain as they were. Their mutual hostility was hurting them both, and was hurting Western Europe in its role in the world.

His message did not fall on deaf ears. Michel Debré had replaced Maurice Couve de Murville as Foreign Minister when the latter had replaced Georges Pompidou as Prime Minister in July 1968. Debré was one of the few people capable of insistently pressing his views on the General. And for years he had been anxious not to let the Franco-British relationship deteriorate too far; what is more, he had wanted to see Britain in the Common Market. For this he had two reasons: firstly to redress the balance with the Germans; secondly to ensure that the Community would not become too supranational in character. By the turn of the year he had convinced the General – much against Couve de Murville's opposition – that he should talk to Soames and see if there was not the chance of taking up again some sort of political exchange of views between the two countries. A meeting was originally fixed for 10 January, but Soames had overdone things in his eagerness to get his feet under the table in Paris, and was ill. But on 4 February Soames was one of a small lunch party at the Elysée, and saw the General privately for an hour or so before and another hour or so after the meal.

We do not have de Gaulle's own side of the run-up to the lunch – he did not live to write that part of his memoirs. In Paris it is said that he was himself not over-eager to go into this conversation, saying to Michel Debré that he did not think much good would come of it. What we do have is Couve de Murville's characteristically sparse account – but then since Couve was a faithful voice of his master, this is as authentic a French government view as we can hope to get.

One could not but be saddened by the growing deterioration in Franco-British relations. De Gaulle was the first to regret it, and sought ways to re-open the dialogue. It could not be on the candidature itself, for the positions had hardened too much for any negotiation on that to be envisaged. One had to raise the debate to its real level – the political future of Europe [la politique européenne]. For de Gaulle, if Britain with her followers entered the Community, the latter would be radically transformed and become a free trade area with arrangements for trade in farm products. That might not nevertheless be such a bad thing. The two governments could talk about it, but on condition they also discussed the resulting political association, in which the four principal partners, France, Britain, Germany and Italy, would necessarily play a key role. In reply to a question from the ambassador on NATO (and not on the Atlantic Alliance) the Head of State added that he did not want the United Kingdom to leave it straight away as a precondition [au préalable], but that if one day there were a truly independent Europe, then there would no longer be any need for a NATO as such, with America's preponderance and her commanding position in it.

The overture to London was clear, on the basis of ideas that France had frequently expressed before and which could not surprise anyone. It was now a matter of putting politics above economics and of talking frankly about them for the first time. This overture was devoid of arrière-pensées, Michel Debré and I know that and can vouch for it; and for that very reason secrecy was asked for until such time as conversations might be started.[1]

There might, in that account, seem at first blush to be two inconsistencies: can you have an initiative on the basis of previously expressed ideas? And, if the dialogue were not on the candidature itself, how could the two governments talk about Britain entering the Community? Both prima facie contradictions disappear, however, when one remembers that the initiative lay in the procedure – bilateral talks – and that this new procedure might well be initiated on the basis of previously expressed ideas, whether de Gaulle's, or the British government's, or both. From that wider conversation about Europe's future there might then follow British entry, not through the mechanics of the Brussels candidature as it had been presented in the past, but as naturally falling into place once agreement had been reached as to the sort of political Europe which it was all about.

Soames returned to the embassy and sent a full telegram to London the same afternoon. In view of the importance he attached to the affair, and to be sure there should be no confusion later as to what had transpired, he decided to revert to a nineteenth-century practice not normal these days, and follow Guizot's precept as given to one of Soames' predecessors and quoted in Satow:

It is said that Lord Normanby, when ambassador at Paris, reproduced a conversation of M. Guizot's, which the latter asserted was incorrect, and he pointed out that the report of a conversation made by a foreign agent can only be regarded as authentic and irrefragable when it has previously been submitted to the person whose language is being reported.[2]

So on Thursday 6 February he presented Bernard Tricot, the Secretary-General of the Elysée, with a copy of his telegram: the

[1] Maurice Couve de Murville, Une Politique Etrangère, Plon, Paris, 1971, pp. 427–8.
[2] Sir Ernest Satow, A Guide to Diplomatic Practice (4th ed.), Longmans, London, 1957, p. 100.

latter according to some accounts could not from what the General had told him confirm the form in which Soames had interpreted the reference to the four principal powers in effect forming an inner council, or the loosening of the Common Market into a free trade area. But he suggested he keep the copy and that Soames should check with Debré, who was then abroad. Debré saw Soames on the Saturday, mentioning the telegram with noises of approval and without any sort of objection or correction at the end of a conversation devoted to other matters.

One could perhaps with hindsight argue that the procedure of a private lunch-time conversation had been less than optimal under the special circumstances. One of the subsequent problems proved to be that London laid great emphasis on the substance of the General's ideas (which were not really new) to the detriment of his willingness to engage in bilateral talks with Britain at all – which would have been a major innovation of form. It may well be that there was a little wool-gathering on the General's part, grand ambiguous sentiments of the kind to be found in his memoirs and press conferences. It may well be too that Christopher Soames asked questions which led the General into paths he had not originally intended to explore, and reported as de Gaulle's cut and dried views what may merely have been rather improvised replies. (This presumably is the implication of Couve de Murville's emphasis in the passage on NATO.) But if this was so, it was up to the French to co-ordinate their diplomatic services some time before the Saturday when Michel Debré met with Soames, to make sure that the impression given was the one they wanted. There is in fact evidence that they were embarrassed at feeling obliged, after the matter had become public a fortnight later, to add to the charges of indiscretion the charge of inaccuracy as well: and that was levied not at Soames' telegram, but at the later Foreign Office summary of it.

At this point, however, the scene shifts to London, where Soames' telegram must have been read at the latest on the Wednesday morning, 5 February. Harold Wilson writes in his memoirs that that week 'we had a report from Christopher Soames, the British ambassador in Paris, who had been granted his long-awaited audience with President de Gaulle. It had been affable and forthcoming, though nothing General de Gaulle said had indicated any greater willingness to see Britain in the Community than he had shown in his long talks with me in Versailles.'[1] Wilson records that neither he, nor, he thought, Soames (nor, as he

[1] Wilson, op. cit., p. 610. Wilson's view of the affair is on pp. 610–13 and 617–18.

later records, Willy Brandt) saw anything new in de Gaulle's ideas on the substance except perhaps for one item that might cause trouble with some of the other five: 'his clear hint that the looser association he proposed would be largely directed by France, Britain, Germany and Italy.'

On the procedure, Wilson records:

He went on to suggest bilateral talks with Britain initially in conditions of great secrecy, on a wide range of economic, monetary, political and defence matters to see whether we could resolve our differences. He said he would like to see a gesture by the British Government proposing that such talks should take place, which he would then welcome. . . . His proposals for bilateral talks I would have regarded as a friendly gesture, subject to our ensuring that they were not used to divide us in either defence or economic affairs from our partners in EFTA and our prospective partners in EEC.[1]

If we were concerned simply with interpreting de Gaulle's mind, this is where we could leave the story. It seems to show readiness on his part, in the context of the changes of the year 1968, to improve his relations with Britain, offer her some alternative political place in Western Europe that might also include EEC membership on the economic side (though the EEC would naturally look different then from the present Community of the Six), and see what would happen. It was, of course, from de Gaulle's point of view a fairly safe thing to do. Just what it really amounted to he did not have to decide until rather later, and in the meantime whether the British accepted or rejected it he would gain some goodwill from trying.

What he had not expected was the sequel, which put an end to all dialogue between the two countries for the remainder of his presidency. To get the story first from the French side (which could see the effect, without being able to disentangle the causes):

Was there a misunderstanding, did London see a trap as people said afterwards (but what trap?), or was it simply that British diplomacy obstinately continued its efforts to drive a wedge [brouiller les cartes] between France and her partners? Whatever the reason, before even replying to our offer or telling us in advance, the Foreign Office sent them a version of the conversation so distorted as to affront them, maintaining for example that de Gaulle wanted a loosening-up of the Community, or that the political association would be confined to the four principal powers. That version was published a few days later, and unleashed a violent press campaign against France.

[1] Wilson, op. cit., p. 610.

It was a 'diplomatic manœuvre' in the best style of bygone centuries. Actually it misled only the naive, and our Brussels colleagues were more embarrassed than irritated with us. But unfortunately the bridges remained cut as badly as they ever had been.[1]

What had happened? In London, the receipt of Soames' telegram caused anxious discussions, both in the Foreign Office and in No. 10 across the way. Harold Wilson was afterwards to blame the Foreign Office for what happened, though as a Prime Minister he was not always – or should not have been – helpless clay in their hands.

The Foreign Secretary and the Office between them in fact had a number of different concerns partly of morality, partly of tactics, partly as to the ends, partly the means. Firstly, Michael Stewart was a convinced supporter of British entry into the EEC and was not prepared to look at any substitutes. He had repeatedly asserted that the only kind of lesser arrangement that Britain could accept would be one that was clearly linked to entry and a prelude to it. In so far as this initiative might lead to entry into the Community, it was obviously to lead into a much looser Community than that of the Six. For de Gaulle this was a fact of life – that, if there were ten, it could no longer be that of the Six but one of Ten – and he was convinced (perhaps it was up to the British to show him wrong) that a wider extension would lead to lesser intensiveness. As far as Michael Stewart was concerned, all de Gaulle had shown was that if de Gaulle really believed that that was all we wanted, then he had not understood what was going on. So this was an unacceptable basis for talks.

Secondly, Michael Stewart had strong views on the political structure of the Community we wanted to enter. It was not one to be dominated by France – nor (if that was what the General seemed now to be retreating towards) by a Franco-British condominium. Britain wanted to enter a Community in which all members had their rightful, constitutional place as befits a democratic body. If de Gaulle thought she wanted to enter to lord it in some sort of directorate over the rest, he was, there too, unfortunately at cross-purposes with her. Thirdly, Michael Stewart was not one of those who believed that entry into the EEC could be secured through Paris directly. To try it that way only meant one was asked for a price one was not prepared to pay – perhaps even a nuclear deal. The only way to get in was to stay close to the

[1] De Murville, op. cit., pp. 428–9.

other five and loyal to the ideal of a Community in which all such decisions have to be taken jointly.

All these three are obviously important points, reflecting credit on the singlemindedness and honour of those who held them. But at the same time one must ask what else they might have expected the General to say. Was it to be expected that an hour with Soames before lunch and an hour after would have converted the General into believing that Luxemburg's place was in its way as important as that of Germany, or that NATO must become a permanent institution in which France would play her part, and that the EEC would remain as it was if it had four new northern members? If not, and if nothing less, however 'affable and forthcoming', would do, then why send in Soames to try to get a dialogue going? In the end it reflected some credit on French cool that they did not try to denounce Soames' attempts to get this conversation as a trap baited for the General to lead him into confidences which could provide ammunition to Britain for denouncing him to the other five.

That, however, leads us on to the questions of procedure. And there, fourthly, the Foreign Office was profoundly suspicious. As one of them said afterwards: 'We had the noose around our neck.' They argued that there must be a trap in it because the French suggested the initiative should seem to come from the British. Yet was the procedure really that fishy? In a sense the initiative had already come from the British in any case. Fundamentally it was they who were asking for a place in Western Europe. Tactically, it was Soames who had been pressing for an audience. Diplomatically it would accord well with French *amour propre* to be seen to accede to rather than to be making a request. And discussion as to who is to initiate a proposal is not such an unusual practice.

Fifthly, there were those in the Foreign Office who believed that the French had before now leaked confidential Franco-British conversations to their partners. They might not do so this time – but the mere implicit threat that they could do so could constitute a form of blackmail. To quote Wilson again, 'They feared – and they were right to emphasize this – that an acceptance by us of the bilateral proposals might be used by the General as an argument, with his colleagues in the Six, that we were not really serious about entry into EEC; indeed that we were having negotiations with him on an entirely separate basis. To do this would not have been out of character, . . .' But Wilson immediately adds what could have substantially removed the threat providing it was done the right way: '. . . and certainly, if we were to enter into bilateral talks, we should have had to make clear to the Five the basis on which we regarded the talks.'[1]

Finally, Michael Stewart himself went rather further. While there were people in the Foreign Office who urged that the French must be consulted or at least warned as to what Wilson might do (and Wilson himself, as we shall see, at one stage said that they had tried to warn the French in advance or at least simultaneously), the Foreign Secretary was adamant not only that the General's proposals must be retailed to the other five, but also that the only honourable course towards the other five was that this should be done unilaterally and without informing the French in advance. As he stated firmly in the House of Commons afterwards: 'It would not have been right to put ourselves in a position where we were in any sense appearing to ask permission to inform our allies of something they had a right to know.' He maintained that 'we never entered into, nor would we have thought it right to enter into, any undertaking to conceal . . . these things from them'.[2] Whether such an undertaking was not implicit in Soames' request for an audience with the General may or may not be another matter. Michael Stewart was later to counter that argument by saying that the General's thinking about the disappearance of NATO and an inner council of the four big powers was a confidence which ought never to have been forced on us – it was as if one of his constituents had confided in him that he intended to commit murder.

What followed was to a certain extent partly an accident of timing. Wilson was due to see Chancellor Kiesinger in Bonn on Wednesday, 12 February, and he relates that 'On the afternoon of my departure for Bonn, Michael Stewart came to see me. . . . It was strongly pressed upon me that if I went to Bonn and did not mention it General de Gaulle might make capital out of that, and succeed in convincing Dr Kiesinger that we were flirting with anti-EEC moves in Paris while supporting EEC legitimacy in Bonn.' Wilson says he did not much like the course of action pressed upon him: 'The way they wanted me to handle it in Bonn seemed designed to discredit the French with their EEC partners, and at the same time present ourselves as a rather priggish little Lord Fauntleroy who had resisted the General's anti-EEC blandishments. I expressed my dislike of the manœuvre, but, as I had to leave within ten minutes, told Michael Stewart that I would

[1] Wilson, op. cit., p. 610.
[2] Hansard, 24 July 1969.

discuss the matter with the senior Foreign Office team who were accompanying me to Bonn.'[1]

But was there really quite such a rush that the whole matter had to be decided on a 'plane, or sitting up late at night in the embassy in Bonn, without cabinet consultation and after only ten minutes with the Foreign Secretary? If so, while sympathizing with the fact that a government has to take a great many decisions simultaneously, one could yet also sympathize with the resignation of the previous Foreign Secretary on 'a really serious issue which has, as you know, been troubling me for some time. It is, in short the way this Government is run, and the manner in which we reach our decisions.'[2] There was a cabinet meeting on Tuesday 11 February, devoted among other things to the farm price review and the Parliament Bill, but there is excellent evidence that several senior cabinet Ministers did not have the problem drawn to their attention until a week after Harold Wilson's return from Bonn. Wilson's account makes it clear that 'we' had had the report the previous week, and not on the Tuesday afternoon. The problem had indeed been under anxious consideration in London – and not without the Prime Minister's knowledge – for six days and a half.

Thus Wilson writes, 'I was anxious to have a fuller assessment from Christopher Soames'. Yet, since transport and telecommunications between the two capitals were uninterrupted throughout that period, one must conclude at the very least that Soames was not sent for to give any such fuller assessment and one may suspect that he received instructions not to come to London. Presumably it was feared that as a political figure in his own right he might seek to influence the use to which his telegram reporting his conversation might be put. And it is, of course, easy for an ambassador to a country to become, as it were, the ambassador for that country and to forget that there are overall policy considerations at stake which are not for him to judge and in comparison with which his position is of subsidiary importance. Wilson concedes that in the event Soames was 'rightly and bitterly upset', though he may have over-estimated the retiring nature of the man in his remark: 'He came over to dine with me at Chequers, but any thoughts he may have had of resigning were dropped.' Having agreed to interrupt his domestic political career to take the Paris embassy and try to shift the log-jam in European affairs, Soames

[1] Wilson, op. cit., pp. 609, 610–11.
[2] Brown, op. cit., p. 169.

seemed determined to bide his time and try again when the opportunity arose. Given that any man had to have a few affairs associated with his name, he was to tell a questioner at the Paris Diplomatic Press Association on 12 March 1969, this was not one of which he need feel ashamed.

It was a pity, from the point of view of the operation on which George Brown had sent Soames out to Paris, that Brown had resigned from the Foreign Secretaryship before Soames ever moved into the Rue de Faubourg Saint-Honoré, so that the partnership which these two colourful characters were hoping to develop in the cause of British entry proved abortive. There is no knowing now how George Brown would have played the ball the General had bowled, but since Brown had persuaded Soames to take the job precisely in order to initiate political conversations, he would hardly have seen the problem in terms described by some as 'a boy scout dilemma'. Was it really impossible to reply immediately that Britain could not be expected to initiate bilateral talks – and that France clearly would not wish to engage in them – without the knowledge of the other five, and that the two countries should therefore forthwith jointly inform the others that they intended to put their heads together? To discuss Europe's political future was after all not tantamount to giving up the attempt to enter the EEC, and that also could have been made clear to the other five. Indeed the reaction of the five only confirmed that they would have welcomed any such development that could start things moving again in Western Europe.

But that was not to be. The rest of the story turned into a muddle of the kind that decisions too long deferred are liable to become. The Foreign Office, having seen the Prime Minister fly off without knowing which way he would decide, had to cover itself against a gamut of contingencies, and warn British ambassadors in the relevant capitals of what might be afoot, telling them to await further instructions. It is at this point that the word 'directorate' appears to have crept into the summary, which was to feed later French accusations of distortion. (What if anything the Foreign Office may at this moment have wired to Paris is, of course, anyone's guess.)

Harold Wilson did not in the event decide till late on the Wednesday morning that he would at least mention the talks-about-talks between de Gaulle and Soames to Kiesinger, so that the German Chancellor could not, if and when he received information later, accuse him of withholding relevant information. He agreed to do it in a few simple sentences without any of the overtones that had been proposed. He continues:

I reached Chancellor Kiesinger's office at four o'clock and asked the Foreign Office team for the brief and anodyne note I had been expecting on the de Gaulle affair. Reading it I found that it was the full works. I made it clear that I was furious; but it was difficult to keep this up in front of the Germans. I therefore made a short statement to Dr Kiesinger of the facts, in as reasoned and unsensational a manner as possible.[1]

The way it actually came over to the Germans was very unfortunate. The Germans got on to their own Paris embassy the same day to get confirmation of the story so as to be able to see it in perspective, but someone from the British embassy in Paris was 'unable to confirm' even the outline of it. The British embassy in Paris had been caught hopping without instructions from London. It was not in fact until around 8.00 p.m. the same day that Christopher Soames was able to arrive at the Quai d'Orsay to see its Secretary-General (who as a result of the late visit, we are informed in a special correction in Le Monde, had to go off to a dinner party in a lounge suit for lack of time to change).[2] Whatever the form in which Soames might have put it, the essence of what he had to say was that the President's confidence had been broken by the Prime Minister, and broken because whatever their Paris ambassador might feel about it, his masters distrusted the President so deeply that they thought he would have betrayed them first.

The final stage of the affair involved its general publication and open mutual recriminations. The French had in any case refused to have any truck with the London meeting of WEU to which Michael Stewart had, on 6–7 February, invited the member states for a discussion of the Middle East on 14 February. Two French newspapers dated Friday 21 February (and published the night before) carried reports of the British diplomatic indiscretion. The Foreign Office that Friday released on an unattributable basis the summary of the Soames telegram that they had sent to British ambassadors. The French countered with accusations of 'diplomatic terrorism', and charges of deliberate distortion (reminiscent of the Ems telegram that had triggered off the Franco-German war of 1870). The coolness between the two countries, which George Brown had sent Soames to thaw, in effect became glacial.

Richard Crossman's hitherto unpublished diary conveys much of the

[1] Wilson, op. cit., p. 611.
[2] 16 March 1969.

atmosphere and also sheds a good deal of light on the affair in the entry dictated on Sunday 23 February:

The first main incident of the week is the de Gaulle explosion.

From my point of view it started when I vaguely noticed in our telegrams there had been an account by the Ambassador, by Christopher Soames, of an interview he had had before lunch with de Gaulle. And at Cabinet on Thursday, in the course of reports by Harold Wilson on his visit to Bonn and Michael Stewart on his visit to the WEU and the manœuvres there, both referred to this conversation. It became clear that Harold Wilson felt compelled to tell Kiesinger in Bonn of the astonishing proposals de Gaulle had made to him, and to pass them on. He felt that in order to prove himself a good boy and a loyal NATO man and a loyal EEC man, he must tell Kiesinger what de Gaulle said to him and of the suggestions de Gaulle made about the future, about the break-up of the EEC and of NATO, and the formulation of the new ideas.

I must admit that during this last Thursday morning I was not attending much. The voice of Michael Stewart is so boringly dull, it goes through your head, it drills into your head, and he goes on and on and on, for twenty minutes or half an hour. He preceded his references to de Gaulle by dealing with four other subjects, and did not suggest it was particularly important. As Roy Jenkins said to me on the 'phone today and as Barbara also said, he has a power of making everything equally unimportant, and he certainly did so on this occasion. Harold Wilson did of course bring it more to one's attention, and then Fred Peart made some observations on whether it was really important for us to make ourselves turn down a proposition for something beyond the Common Market, but he was hardly listened to, so that is how I first heard about it discussed at the Thursday Cabinet.

Well, on Friday evening it became clear that in the course of Friday mid-day a major decision had been taken, and that decision was that the Foreign Office would announce formally that the conversations had taken place and give their version of them. But this of course produced a major Anglo-French crisis which went on booming along in the Saturday and Sunday papers. The decision by the British Foreign Office and the British Foreign Secretary to announce a top secret conversation is of course quite distinct from the decision of Harold Wilson on going to Bonn to tell Kiesinger about it. It's intelligible that he should fear that if he didn't tell Kiesinger and the French did our whole position would be undermined and this was the trap which de Gaulle had laid for him. I don't so much blame Harold for at least telling Kiesinger something about it. But I was very interested as to why on earth on Friday afternoon, though no suggestion had been made to the Cabinet that it should be published, the decision had been taken to publish it. And I took the opportunity this morning, when I was ringing up Harold Wilson about the successor to Stephen Swingler, of asking him about it. And he said: 'Well you know, after we got back from the funeral' (you see, he and I were at Stephen Swingler's funeral at 12.30 and got back into London about 1.30 from the funeral) 'after I got back from the funeral, just before I went off to Ipswich I got this proposal from the Foreign Office to publish in view of the French leaks and we said "Maybe . . .". Of course I didn't want to lay a trap for de Gaulle, but maybe I was wrong.'

I said: 'My God. Do you mean that is how it was fixed?'

He said: 'Yes. I gave my consent then, I am not so sure it was wise.' And then I said, 'What will Christopher Soames do about it? He's coming back today.' And Harold said, 'Well, he'll be in a terrible fury because he will think his honour has been impugned.' And then he explained how he, Harold, had told Kiesinger before Soames had got permission from the French Foreign Office, although the plan had been for Soames to see Alphand on the evening before Harold talked to Kiesinger. It didn't work that way because the interview in Paris was postponed until the next morning and so technically we put ourselves in the wrong by telling the Germans before we got the leave of the French. And now this had been followed up by an announcement by the Foreign Office of the content of the conversations. No wonder the French talk about a crisis.

In the end as it happened the affair did not do lasting harm. President de Gaulle relinquished his office within three months, Harold Wilson within eighteen, and both sides decided to start afresh. (Perhaps neither felt that they had come out of this affair in the best of all possible lights.) On the contrary, the episode came to serve President Pompidou's entourage as a stalking horse to defend British entry in the face of some Gaullist reproaches. But its mythical value today does not on the other hand solve our historical problem. Did de Gaulle – or did he not – start steering French policy into the curve which finally led to the Treaty of Accession?

The answer is partly determined by how one interprets such metaphors. What one can perhaps conclude is this. De Gaulle had from the beginning been aware of the cross-Channel implications of the integration of the Six. (Pompidou – for his own purposes of course – related in 1971 how de Gaulle had years before said to him of the EEC '*Ça va nous brouiller avec les Anglais*'.) He was not so obtuse as to fail to see what a really 'European-minded' Britain could add to the construction of a powerful European-minded Europe to offset the larger power of the USA. Like a good politician, therefore, he never said 'never'. What he said was that the British were not ripe, and that the Continentals themselves, in their own construction, were not yet securely enough established to be able to absorb the British without transforming their Community totally. So the British must not come in too early. In particular, the agricultural policy really had to be tied up first before the British came in.

Yet, at the same time, the British must not come into the West European political equation too late either: while de Gaulle himself was alive France could prevail in the Community, but time was on Germany's side, and German power was growing. The events of 1968 speeded up the shift in the relative weight of the two powers, Germany and France. No harm, therefore, perhaps – even if little good could yet come of it – in making a friendly gesture to a new ambassador, in thinking aloud into the future, and, if bilateral talks did begin, in showing the other five that France could talk to Britain, was willing to do so, and was not married exclusively to them. Particularly since, tactician as he was, it would cost him nothing, and just what it was he meant by it he could always decide in the light of later requirements.

Had the Soames affair been merely one of diplomatic ineptitude, even new evidence on what happened would not justify lengthy discussion. In fact, however, the affair did point up several factors that were to take on greater significance later. On the French side, it displayed the unease with which influential people in Paris – even under de Gaulle, and perhaps including de Gaulle – saw the almost pathological enmity between the two countries. On the side of the five, who were embarrassed and unhappy at London's behaviour, it once more demonstrated their concern to have this enmity bridged, even by bilateral procedures. Competent observers in Paris believe, indeed, that to gain credit with the other five was one of the General's motivations. He may well have envisaged a settlement with the British as the price to be paid for the agricultural settlement which he needed in Brussels – precisely the bargain that his successor was to strike at The Hague. And in Britain it illustrated – apart from anything more episodic about individuals – the conflict between the two very different lines of policy: on the one side that of talking – without the French, if need be (as in WEU) – to the other five, and hoping that France's partners would twist her arm into letting Britain in; and on the other side that of seeking secret bilateral negotiations with the French behind the backs, if necessary, of the rest. We shall encounter the two strategies again in considering the bid that was finally successful.

2 Pompidou Keeps his Options Open

Le propre de l'action politique, je l'ai dit à propos d'autre chose, c'est de se garder les mains libres, et croyez que je tâcherai de me les garder!

Georges Pompidou

The Domestic Constraints

Charles de Gaulle's resignation from the presidency of France occurred only days before the twentieth anniversary of the Council of Europe on 5 May 1969. The celebrations of the date held in London were notable for the jubilation of the 'Europeans' at his departure and the reiterated determination of the British government to accede to the EEC. In the election campaign that ensued for the French presidency the 'Europeans' (who had very largely supported Lecanuet in 1965) rallied to the flag of the honest, previously almost unknown and totally uninspiring Acting President Alain Poher, who among other worthy liberal causes championed Britain's entry into the EEC.

The Gaullists naturally put up as their candidate Georges Pompidou, de Gaulle's Prime Minister from 1962 until July 1968, when – after his cool competence at the time of the May events – the General placed him 'in the reserve of the Republic'. 'I hope', de Gaulle had written to him in his letter of dismissal, 'that you will remain in readiness to carry out any mission and to take up any office which the nation may one day call on you to assume.' Georges Pompidou's public attitude to British entry was proclaimed less forthrightly than Alain Poher's, but it was not hostile. Within a week of the resignation – be it because that was what he already really believed, because he had not yet found his feet in international affairs and did not want to have to fight in defence of the General's foreign policies, because he needed electoral support, or for a combination of such reasons – he declared his agreement with the policy of Giscard d'Estaing's Independent Republicans (who had commanded some 61 seats in the Assembly after the 1968 general election): this policy included both the maintenance of the Atlantic alliance and the enlargement of the EEC. On 9 May 1969 Pompidou told the National Central Committee of the Gaullist party that he would like to see Europe 'enlarged once the conditions for thi, are achieved by our potential partners' – still a cautious formulations but at least cast in a positive (if conditional) rather than a negative form. And he called Britain's exclusion by President de Gaulle 'dramatic' – as if to imply that he was less likely to indulge in such gestures.

Alain Poher obtained 23% against Georges Pompidou's 44% of the votes cast in the first ballot, and 42% against Pompidou's 58% in the run-off in June. On the surface Gaullism appeared to have obtained the chance of continuity beyond the General's reign. It remained to be seen how far anyone but de Gaulle could carry it off, and how far Pompidou for that matter would even wish to do so once he was firmly in the saddle. He himself defined his overall policy as a combination of continuity and 'ouverture' – change. That was a platitude. What he refused to say was where the change would come, in what direction, to what extent, and when.

Let us note that, on taking office, Pompidou had to reckon with quite definite handicaps. He was put up by the Gaullists, and the Gaullists formed the backbone of his support in the country. Yet he was not by nature or record a natural Gaullist himself at all. He had stood aside from de Gaulle's historic struggle for France against the Nazis. He had not met de Gaulle until that struggle was over and the liberated country had to be administered. He was not cast in the heroic soldier's, but in the peasant's and banker's mould. His concern might well be less with the glory of France, more with the well-being of the French: he would be less prone to the dramatic gesture, more to the calculation of economic costs and benefits. Had de Gaulle not chosen him, he would hardly have chosen de Gaulle. And that fact was very well understood by the historic Gaullists, who knew he was beholden to them for his election and were determined to see that he did not betray them once they had put him into the Elysée.

They seemed at the outset to be fairly well placed to do so. With 280 out of 487 seats in the Assembly (the result of the 1968 vote for stability) they felt able to block departures from orthodoxy, and made it certainly more convenient for Pompidou to adopt at least the language of continuity. Though the General himself had declared that he would not interfere again in French politics except in time of crisis (and had absented himself in Ireland during the election campaign), there were always a few people willing to spread the latest word from Colombey in Paris. The fundamentalist wing of the party founded a group to keep the rest on the straight and narrow under the title *Présence et Action du Gaullisme*. In November 1969 some became associated in a *Mouvement pour l'Indépendance de l'Europe* determined to preserve the

General's attitude towards the Anglo-Saxons. It has even been argued that the municipal elections of March 1971 (in which nearly 40,000 candidates were standing) were a date the French government preferred to have behind it before seeking a breakthrough in the Brussels negotiations. However that may be, there were certainly faithful Gaullists looking critically over Pompidou's shoulder in the early months of his presidency.

What was then not yet clear was how the balance of the institutions of the Fifth Republic would shift once de Gaulle was gone. Some have argued that de Gaulle constructed the constitution to fit himself. Others have argued that he did not need it: he constructed it to fit his successor. Whatever the intention, the effect has indeed been that France remains under a system of government obviously *sui generis*, but still far closer to the presidential than the parliamentary model. The distinction soon came to be made between the presidential and the parliamentary coalition. The Gaullists could not have elected Pompidou on their own. It had taken Giscard's Independent Republicans and the Centrists of Jacques Duhamel and Maurice Schumann to give Pompidou an absolute majority in the second round. But it also soon became apparent that once elected, and after getting the feel of the system, President Pompidou was no less dominant over the French political scene than de Gaulle had been – indeed was sometimes more in charge than de Gaulle had been, not least because he used a 'low-profile', rather less abrupt and subtler political style.

On the European front it was immediately noted that in the government he chose to install under him Pompidou put into key posts three men with established European leanings: Valéry Giscard d'Estaing at the Ministry of Finance; Jacques Duhamel at Agriculture; and, at the Quai d'Orsay, Maurice Schumann, 'the most European of the Gaullists, the most Gaullist of the Europeans', an Anglophile who looked back to the years spent in London during the war as the 'Voice of Free France' as perhaps the happiest of his life. Yet not too much must be made of the effects of these three appointments. Duhamel as Minister of Agriculture was hardly likely to welcome in the British except on the toughest of material terms. Schumann, however much happier he might feel being nice than being beastly to the British, was to prove an executor rather than a formulator of policy. At most his appointment marked a change of style in foreign relations: after the dour, tough precision of Maurice Couve de Murville (who was dropped altogether) and Michel Debré (who took on Defence, which he could hardly refuse), the genial, talkative Schumann presented an image of good fellowship travelling to all the neighbouring capitals and many a more distant land. In any case all three men were really put there for reasons of domestic, not foreign policy: Giscard, in spite of his difficult relations with Pompidou, because he had an independent parliamentary base within the Gaullist coalition, Duhamel and Schumann because some of the leaders of the Centre (which had by no means always supported de Gaulle, and indeed walked out of his government in 1962) needed to be brought in to consolidate the parliamentary majority after the presidential election.

The idea of a European summit conference was in the air during the election campaign. But it was not until some weeks after his victory that Georges Pompidou, on 10 July 1969, committed himself to it. No such summit could possibly have avoided dealing with the issue of the Community's enlargement. Had Pompidou not wished to put himself into a position where he would have to discuss that issue with the other five, he should not have called for a summit: if the summit was 'imposed' on him as a condition of electoral support, or as one element in an agreement on how to form a presidential majority, then here already was an internal constraint on him which could help balance the Gaullist vigilantes. In other words by entering into an electoral alliance which on the issue of British entry implied 'ouverture' rather than 'continuité' and by honouring that alliance with the appointment of Centrist Ministers, Pompidou was – intentionally or not – already beginning to give himself a margin of manœuvre between opposing wings of his own majority, a margin he could hope to widen and then exploit with time.

The Prime Minister, however, was a Gaullist. Jacques Chaban-Delmas had led the Gaullist group in the National Assembly in the mid-'fifties, held office as a Gaullist in the Fourth Republic first as Minister of Works under Mendès-France, then as Minister of Defence in the cabinets of Mollet and Gaillard, and then presided over the National Assembly of the Fifth Republic until Pompidou, in 1969, moved him to the Hôtel Matignon. The new Prime Minister was a keen supporter of Pompidou during de Gaulle's last months as President after Pompidou had been relieved of the premiership. It was generally thought that Chaban-Delmas was favourable to British entry. Mayor of Bordeaux since 1947 – like so many other French politicians, he retained his local functions though busy on the national level – he comes from a region where the British are liked, in any case.

Yet if any appointment had nothing to do with foreign policy it was his. 'The Prime Minister never meddles in foreign affairs. Indeed it's quite embarrassing. When we want him to visit some foreign country, he tells us he is far too busy doing his job to go abroad.' There is no prize for guessing to which country's foreign office the speaker of that sentence belonged. Perhaps indeed one must beware in the case of the Fifth Republic of translating *premier ministre* as anything but 'first Minister' – the man in charge of relations with the party, the parliament, and (supervising the Minister of the Interior) with the people, absorbing domestic pressures, administering the government at home, to free the President for greater concentration on foreign affairs. 'Pompidou himself hardly ever opened his mouth in cabinet on foreign affairs when he was Prime Minister', one of his colleagues related later. As for Chaban-Delmas it seems that indeed there was at one time a danger of his becoming involved in the British entry issue. February 1971 was the time of the Franco-British rugby international at Twickenham. Chaban-Delmas let it be known that he wanted to come over and see it. Downing Street replied that he was of course welcome, and must stay and use the opportunity to have a chat. But the unfortunate former wing-forward had to be content with watching the match on television. The President of the Republic signified that he was not to go.

In his book *British Politics and European Unity*, Robert Lieber set himself a theoretical task – that of verifying the proposition that 'politicization' causes a decline in the role of sectional pressure groups. Politicization he defines as an increase in the perception and treatment of an issue as one of major national importance; it is indicated by the issue being handled by primarily political ministries, the involvement of the broader public, and the active participation of political parties.[1] However convincing his conclusions may be in the British case, the Fifth Republic does not fit very easily into this kind of treatment. The involvement of the broader public was minimal, and the participation of the political parties marginal. To that extent the issue was 'non-politicized'. Yet the handling at the highest political level was complete, and the role of the pressure groups almost non-existent. To that extent the issue was 'superpoliticized'. Foreign policy in other words is regarded in the Fifth Republic as being of such major national importance (Lieber's definition of politicization) that it cannot be left to the politicians – nor to the political parties and the public. It was and still

[1] Robert J. Lieber, *British Politics and European Unity – Parties, Elites and Pressure Groups*, University of California Press, Berkeley, 1970, pp. 10–13.

predominantly remains the prerogative of the President, regarded almost as being 'above' politics.

At the same time the problem of British entry was no longer as capital an issue of France's foreign policy as it had been. The difference between being and not being a member of the EEC obviously has far greater consequences for a country than the difference between being in an EEC of six or an EEC of ten members. It clearly mattered to the French farmers on just what terms Britain was to come in, if she were to come in. The *Confédération Générale du Travail*, following the Communist line, in so far as it took up any attitude at all was hostile to British entry. The other unions were perhaps not especially interested, but rather favourable: the inclusion of a strong British labour movement in the EEC might help keep business interests in check and revive the social thrust of the whole enterprise. The *Patronat*, which had made detailed studies in 1961–62, did not really trouble to go into the issues involved again this time: broadly speaking they felt that if they could not simply survive, but do extremely well with their exports in competition with German industry, there was nothing to be frightened of in Britain's entry. Indeed, the large firms could see distinct advantages. The *Petits et Moyens Entreprises* were more concerned, since some of their members in certain sectors could expect to suffer. But few of the so-called pressure groups appear to have made any public representations on the issue. They may on average be regarded as having blessed the outcome with benign neglect.

As far as the National Assembly was concerned‹ as early as November 1969 the foreign affairs debate already revealed a certain change of emphasis. Maurice Schumann's speech remained well within the Gaullist orthodoxy in everything it said – though not perhaps in everything that it omitted. Michel Boscher, as loyal a Gaullist as one could wish, talked of British entry as an accepted fact that France could not oppose for long. Jean de Broglie, chairman of the Foreign Affairs Committee, presented a report in the name of his Committee later in the month asking

If it is in France's interests to secure for Europe an economic potential that allows her to raise herself to the American level, how could one imagine a European currency without the pound sterling, a capital market without the contribution of the City, a Europe of computers without the contribution of the most complex and advanced which are of British manufacture?

And he was quite unequivocal in his pronouncement that 'It is in the political, strategic and economic interest of France that the entry of Britain should come about'.[1]

His report spelled out these interests in detail. As far as the political side was concerned, stereotyped rhetoric took over:

The democratic and parliamentary tradition anchored in the British mentality provides a guarantee for the Community's future that our concepts of individual human dignity will be psychologically reinforced, and that the chances of freedom will have greater eternity in the West. The vagaries [la houle] of the Latin, the sometimes disquieting romanticism of the Germanic spirit will find in contact with the English character a reinforcement that must be regarded as beneficial and reassuring.[2]

But there was also a hardheaded consideration of where British influence would be a lesser evil:

A proper understanding of our interests leads us very much rather to note that in the end the United Kingdom's influence would be much more equivocal and uncontrollable [insaisissable] outside than inside the Community. . . . Britain's non-entry into the European whole would . . . lead the United Kingdom back into the American orbit from which one could never prise her loose, and would induce such a shock and disappointment among some of our partners that the Community would be permanently weakened by it. The notion of Europe's independence would become even more removed from reality.[3]

Maurice Schumann endorsed de Broglie's speech as 'one which could be already a foreign minister's' and it was not surprising that a guardian of the holy grail, de Gaulle's brother-in-law Jacques Vendroux, found it necessary to reiterate:

The upholding of French standpoints is not only a matter of intention but also, and especially, one of firmness. . . . The adventure of broadening the Common Market must not be embarked upon before the completion and consolidation of the Europe of the Six.[4]

But the Gaullist orthodoxy on the point was vanishing fast. By spring 1970 the 'completion' if not the 'consolidation' was after all agreed. Thereafter there never really developed any debate in France on the

[1] Doc. 865 annexed to the National Assembly official proceedings of 5 November 1969, p. 13.
[2] Op. cit., p. 12.
[3] Op. cit., pp. 12–13.
[4] The Times, 6 November 1969.

abandonment of the stand de Gaulle had taken so dramatically and repeatedly.

Of course the diehards maintained their position. But the very fact that there was a Gaullist President with a Gaullist Prime Minister at the helm undermined their practical opportunities of resistance. As François Bruel put it:

There is growing anxiety among several of the personalities who follow diplomatic affairs that Messrs Pompidou and Debré are committing one of the most dramatic errors of judgment in history. . . . Europe and France would fall into a state of complete dependence, through the agency [*truchement*] of Great Britain acting on behalf of the United States.

Bruel added

Who could have imagined any such total reversal of French foreign policy?. . . No other parliamentary majority, whether under François Mitterand or under Alain Poher, could have gone to such lengths in the opposite direction from General de Gaulle's desire to save France and Europe from such a fate.[1]

The counter-arguments were summarized, just as the 1971 Paris summit was being fixed, by Jean-Marcel Jeanneney, who had been three times a Minister under de Gaulle, and who set out 'three reasons against Britain's entry into the EEC',[2] if the latter was to be a 'European Europe'. The first was the fear of economic dependence on the USA if Britain were to join. At first sight this seems a paradoxical argument, considering how much stronger the Community might become through enlargement. But enlargement, Jeanneney argued, would provoke a reaction. Third countries, the USA in particular, 'have – not without some regret – been prepared to put up with the very moderate protectionism of the Six. They could hardly tolerate that of an enlarged Community. . . . They will seek to make it into a free trading one, and one must fear that, thanks to the many different means of pressure the USA has at its disposal, they will succeed.' The result would be asymmetrical, making Europe incapable of conducting her own economic policy and in a slump laying her open to foreign competition with disastrous economic and political results.

The second reason Jeanneney cited was that Britain would impose on the enlarged Community her own close links with the USA, 'for Britain would have a determining weight in the Community precisely

[1] *Le Télégramme Economique*, 26 April 1971.
[2] *Le Monde*, 5 May 1971.

because of America's support for her and also because of the great skill her diplomats have always had to divide and rule'.

Thirdly (under the subtitle 'The French language is threatened') he argued that 'in the Community of the Six, no national language can supplant the others . . . thus the linguistic originality and plurality of Europe are preserved, which are an integral part of her culture and contribute to the international linguistic balance which is gravely threatened already. . . . It is essential that Europeans should express their attitudes to life in the languages which are their own.' In all three ways, therefore, France had to guard against getting drawn into 'a vast Atlantic conglomerate, whose control will be out of our hands, and in which we may well fear that our interests will be sacrificed and European civilization in the end dissolve.'

Brilliant in its dialectics though the article was – and it deserves to be read in full (it contains on the one side long-range threats of a Communist take-over in reaction against dependence on America, and on the other side recognition, all too rare anywhere so far, that supranational institutions might well come to serve Britain's interests and policies) – it was the last shot across the bows before the summit. Couve de Murville and Jeanneney found by this time that there were few to maintain the old stand that had determined French policy right through the 'sixties: indeed Jeanneney was to resign from the party later in 1971. The General himself was now dead, Germany in that same month of May flaunted her independence of France and of the freshly agreed steps towards monetary union by floating the Deutschmark, and the tendency of the United States to turn inwards on its domestic problems was becoming more and more apparent. From May 1968 until May 1971 the fallacies on which Gaullist heroics had been based had relentlessly been exposed one by one by events. By the end of the month British entry was taken as a *fait accompli* and hardly a voice raised in protest against the warmth of the Paris welcome.

The domestic limits on Georges Pompidou's freedom of manœuvre were, therefore, eroded during the first two years of his presidency. Probably they were even at the outset not in fact as strong as he feared and supposed – the Gaullist vigilantes did not have either the leverage under de Gaulle's constitution nor the cohesion and driving-force without de Gaulle's leadership that could have opposed Pompidou effectively. They proved men of straw. With his ministerial team more in favour than de Gaulle's had been, a majority of his parliament apparently willing to be in favour at quite an early stage, the interest groups for what they were worth on balance neutral to favourable, and public opinion vaguely favourable also, by May 1971 it was getting at least as easy for him to say 'yes' as to say 'no'.

Nor was this simply the effect of the passage of time and the evolution of outside events. Certainly time was needed to turn the corner in domestic politics. But Pompidou himself had both adapted to and in turn affected the temper of the French political system on the issue. At the outset the tough negotiating position had reassured the Gaullist traditionalists: a softer position would have invited domestic criticism. By the end, the danger of criticism was more on the other side, from those who might have thought French diplomacy too obstructive: and the Paris summit disarmed them in their turn. It was, in terms of internal politics, a very accomplished operation to free himself by judicious timing from the domestic constraints of the past. The decision could be his, and his alone, and it could be taken in almost purely foreign policy terms.

The Road to The Hague

In January 1968, Georges Pompidou had made a bet with a friend, for £10 in sterling, that de Gaulle's second veto would soon be forgotten and before the year was out the Common Market would have got going again. But Britain did not just go away. The other five did not give up trying to get her in. The Common Market's progress was severely held up right through 1968 and 1969, to the point where *Der Spiegel* in Germany just before the Hague summit devoted the core of its issue to 'the break-up of the Common Market'.[1] Progress in European integration had reached stalemate: Pompidou lost his bet, and no doubt paid up.

In considering his own possible future foreign policy, during that period from summer 1968 to summer 1969 when the General placed him 'in the Republic's reserve', Georges Pompidou thus had to consider how far this pressing desire of France's partners – which he had so underestimated before – now had to be met to allow the Community to reach the end of its transition period as planned on 1 January 1970. He seems early on to have come to the conclusion that, having lost his bet, he had to draw the consequences from the facts of the situation. It was during this period, when he had a small staff in the Boulevard de Latour-Maubourg, that a British diplomat came to see him, and – whether to differentiate himself from the General who had dismissed

---

[1] *Der Spiegel*, 24 November 1969, pp. 124–48.

him, whether touting for support (a most unlikely hypothesis), whether in anticipation of the electoral alliance that was to give him his presidential majority or whether out of conviction – Georges Pompidou was categoric in the winter of 1968–69 that, if he were President, he would try to bring Britain into the Community. He said the same thing quietly to French observers at the same time.

Later, immediately after his election, when friends wrote to him to urge him not to miss the opportunity of bringing Britain into the EEC, they had an oral message back saying it was a chance that he did not intend to miss. Well before the Hague summit, the British embassy in Paris was convinced that, when Pompidou said there was no objection of principle, they were on firm ground in believing that he meant what he said. It was not a feeling that was shared in London. On the night of the breakthrough in Brussels in May, a British diplomat was heard to declare that the Brussels negotiations had been difficult, but more difficult still had been those of the British embassy with the British government to convince the latter that Pompidou would not deliberately aim at producing a breakdown in the attempt.

On his election the first task facing Pompidou in European policy was, of course, not the enlargement of the Community, but the tying up of the common farm policy and the conclusion of a definitive settlement of the issue of financing it. Yet his partners, who went to see him in Paris in the early weeks of his presidency, Brandt and Luns chief among them, impressed on him the need for enlargement. It became clear that a deal of the one for the other was possible, desirable for both sides, and thus perhaps even inevitable. At his first press conference, on 10 July 1969, Pompidou endorsed the call (already voiced, among others, by Brandt before the French elections were over) for a summit conference. This had to be held when the Germans, too, had gone to the polls, as they were due to do at the end of September. And on enlargement he declared: 'We have no objection of principle against a possible accession by the United Kingdom. But we do think it right that the Six should first reach agreement amongst themselves.' By November 1969, he was saying that he actually wished to see a negotiation opened, while Maurice Schumann went further, saying 'We don't simply accept the opening of negotiations, we also hope that they will succeed'.[1] The precondition remained: the agricultural policy had to be settled once and for all before the negotiations with Britain opened. 'Completion' had to come before 'enlargement'.

[1] *L'Express*, 24 November 1969.

The logic here was perfectly overt. On the one side, a continuity of vocabulary with his former master's voice, and on the other side, a gesture of 'opening' towards the other five, and towards Britain, without which the European log-jam could hardly be resolved. In late 1969, it must be remembered, the financial regulations for agriculture needed re-negotiation: and it was the French who wanted it most badly. De Gaulle had sometimes been able to get what he wanted by blackmail. No one, on the other hand, thought Pompidou quite mad enough to carry out the sort of threat with which de Gaulle was willing to play (and with which he had finally and perhaps half-deliberately committed political suicide). 'A long era of visionaries – Winston Churchill, Charles de Gaulle, Adenauer, Stalin and Kennedy – has just come to an end. The hour of the realists has now come', as Arthur Conte put it in the National Assembly debate.[1] And however much Maurice Schumann argued that there could be no question of a deal, since completion was merely the fulfilment of a contract sealed in 1957, while enlargement was something else, in substance the other five to some extent had France over the barrel.

The other five, in fact, largely shared the agnosticism not to say occasional scepticism of the British government as to the sincerity of the French public declarations. One can see why. President de Gaulle himself had declared in May 1967 that there never had been a veto, and that there would not be one then. That had not prevented him from breaking up the negotiations in 1963 and stopping them from ever starting in 1967. A veto by any other name can be equally effective and indeed less expensive in terms of goodwill from one's partners. So what the five required of France was a convincing show of sincerity. The timing of the two elements was such that the other five had to deliver before the French. The risk was that, after having obtained a financial regulation which under the Treaty had to be pretty final in character, the French would then take up an attitude so stiff that they could not absolutely be accused of a new veto – but that they would force the British to draw back from unacceptable conditions, and thus have it both ways. Moreover time was getting short. The Rome Treaty had set 1 January 1970 as the date by which, the twelve years of transition over, all the common policies were to be in operation. And by the time the summit meeting could actually take place, it was 1 December 1969 – just a month away from the end of the transition period.

[1] *The Times*, 6 November 1969.

In the Ridderzaal at The Hague Pompidou's not very lengthy opening speech in which he said the entry negotiations must be taken up 'in a positive spirit, but without losing sight of the interests of the Community and of its members' fell flat. *Le Figaro*, having somewhat prematurely featured the headline 'Pompidou Stars at The Hague', had rapidly to change its tune. 'A de Gaulle without the same talent', was an Italian diplomat's reaction.[1] *The Times* called it 'deplorable'.[2] It was eclipsed by the formidable list of precise demands put together by 'Willy Brandt's eager beavers' – to quote a French diplomat's view of the asymmetry between the opening statements of the two men, both appearing for the first time in their lives as heads of state or of government in the international arena.

Brandt's speech, from the British point of view, was notable in that here the Germans were playing the German card themselves. Addressing himself explicitly to Pompidou, Brandt enumerated four reasons for broadening the Community: first because (a very lightly veiled threat) 'experience has shown that putting off the question of enlargement threatened to paralyse the Community': in other words – no financial regulation without a promise of fair play for the applicants. Second, because enlargement would be useful

at a time when we are endeavouring to bring East and West more closely together. . . . Third, the Community must grow beyond the Six if it wants to hold its own economically and technologically with the giants and to meet its world responsibilities. And I do not hesitate to add a fourth argument: anyone who fears that the economic strength of the Federal Republic of Germany could cause an imbalance within the Community ought to be in favour of the enlargement for this very reason.

Piet de Jong, the Dutch Prime Minister, then proposed that enlargement should be discussed first. Pompidou, in pained surprise, countered that farming must come first. This was agreed – everyone knew by this time that that was France's price for lifting the veto. But Brandt and de Jong countered with an attempt partially to redress the timing problem. They would agree to sign a financial regulation before the end of the year: submission to parliamentary ratification, however, might not be very immediate. It might – they implied – depend on the spirit France showed in the further discussion of the enlargement issue.

That night, after Queen Juliana's banquet, Brandt and Pompidou

[1] *L'Express*, 6 December 1969.
[2] Editorial of 3 December 1969.

had a private half-hour session together, and next morning Pompidou struck a totally different note. The journalists naturally concluded that there had been some tough talking not far removed from arm-twisting at the Huis ten Bosch palace. But French diplomats insist that the Monday afternoon speech had been a raising, not an answering of questions, as became the convenor and opener of a conference of that kind – above all if trained in the French academic tradition, which tries to see problems in their context and their wider relationships before getting down to shopping lists of detailed solutions. It was in this speech ('to round off' that of the afternoon before) that Pompidou pulled various rabbits out of his hat on the subject of 'deepening' and notably called for a complete economic and monetary union, plans for it to be agreed by the end of 1970. He added that he was favourably inclined to the enlargement of the Community, and that the Six should get their common position on this agreed 'in the most rapid, active and positive manner'. The long final communiqué was drafted in only five hours (Pompidou was particularly concerned that the French delegation should not go too far in the wording on economic and monetary union). Victory all round had been snatched from the jaws of disaster.

By the same token, however, the options were beginning to narrow. Until The Hague it might have been just possible to try to continue broadly, though less rigidly, along the straight paths originally paved by the General. After The Hague, Pompidou had lost that corset. It began to become as difficult for him to veto as not to veto (and possibly more so). The probability of an outright veto was thus reduced. But that still left open the choice between two very different negotiating strategies: one that could have come close to blocking entry *de facto*, insisting on terms so stiff that the British would give up themselves, and the other that of actually having them in.

France's Negotiating Strategy

For Britain there was thus quite a valley to be traversed between the Hague summit in December 1969 and the Paris summit in May 1971. President Pompidou, in a television address to the nation on 15 December, stated the position of his government very fairly. He emphasized that the Hague summit had 'demonstrated the sincerity of the statements I made on taking office when I announced that France would not veto British entry into the Common Market'. (He also stressed that he wished to see 'the traditional links with our American friends and allies' drawn closer – hardly a Gaullist turn of phrase.) But at the same time he threw the onus of what was to happen on to the British. 'I hope the negotiations . . . will prove that Britain really is determined to turn towards Europe.'

His doubts on the matter were not set at rest by the publication in February 1970 of the British White Paper setting out some estimates of the costs of entry – which had *L'Aurore*, a staunch supporter of Britain on the issue, asking in a two-column headline: 'These English – What do they really want?' When he was questioned in the National Press Club in Washington during his official visit to the United States, Pompidou recalled Winston Churchill's phrase which de Gaulle had quoted so often – when Britain had to choose between the Continent and the open seas, she would always choose the open seas. 'Right up to the last moment', he said, 'we cannot be sure of the British determination to enter the Market.'[1]

If that was true from the French standpoint, it was equally true from the British point of view that right until the last moment one could not be sure whether France would allow Britain in or whether she was determined, by one means or another, to keep her out. French diplomacy in fact remained profoundly ambiguous from Pompidou's election in summer 1969 until the spring of 1971. There was no telling whether Pompidou had made up his mind against British entry but resolved to proceed more subtly than the General, whether he was reserving judgment, or whether he had already decided that Britain had to be admitted, but was determined to exact the maximum price.

What was not clear then, but is clear now, was that not only was the world ignorant of his intentions, but that even some of his top advisers were, for most of this period, uncertain in their own minds as to what he really wanted. He is a man, they agree, who plays his cards very close to his chest. He is a man who is slow to take decisions. He talked tough even in the most restricted negotiating councils at the Elysée – but then he had to, as his Foreign Minister was always anxious to please his partners. Yet his closest collaborators also say they never felt they were actually negotiating to fail.

Once the issue of agricultural finance had been settled between the Six in April 1970, and the EEC had thus – even if four months late – successfully completed its twelve-year transition period, one of the preconditions for enlargement had at last been fulfilled. The system had been consolidated in such a form that new members would have

[1] *The Times*, 25 February 1970.

the greatest difficulty in going back on it. This was a matter of general principle. In addition, and in particular, the French had tied down their partners to a system of finance that would for a long time involve transfers in France's favour by helping to pay for agriculture out of the superior productivity of the Community's industries. The other tasks, in early 1970, were therefore twofold: first, to agree on the conditions that the applicant countries had to fulfil in the negotiations with the Six (and the forms the negotiations were to take); and second, simultaneously to continue the Community's progress without slowing down to wait for the new members to catch up and get on board. The fact that such continued impetus might pre-empt choices which the candidate countries might wish to see made differently was at the least irrelevant, and at the most a bonus in that it would force the candidates to give further proofs of Community virtue beyond those demanded at the time of their application.

At The Hague, Pompidou had non-committally let it be known that he did not think the definition by the Six of their common negotiating position – his prerequisite for the opening of negotiations with the candidates – should take more than six months. The French negotiators did not attempt to filibuster. What they did do was to try to obtain the toughest possible terms. In 1961 the Macmillan government had put its head into a rather dangerous noose with the so-called 'London declaration' – which stipulated that all the partners of EFTA must be granted satisfactory terms by the EEC from the same date, as a pre-condition of Britain's (or any other EFTA state's) entry into the EEC. It was a curious notion, which would have given Portugal or Austria a veto that no one thought of according to Australia or India. In 1966–67 the Wilson government had made it clear that the London declaration no longer obtained. But in 1970 the French tried to revive it in reverse, claiming that no state should be accepted as a member unless it proved possible to make satisfactory arrangements for all the other EFTA members at the same time. That was a condition they in the event could not get agreed by their partners. But they raised the sterling problem, to which we shall return in a moment; and they were glad to agree to a fisheries regulation that suited their deep sea fishermen but not their inshore fishing fleets, because they knew that it would cause far greater difficulties for the British and the Norwegians, and would therefore be another trump card should they want to raise the obstacles so high that Britain would jib at clearing them.

The Quai d'Orsay negotiated hard and was determined not only to throw no cards away but to pick up any more they could get to make their position even tougher. No wonder that in London and in the capitals of the other five there were strong suspicions that Pompidou wanted to remain loyal to de Gaulle's political objectives, but felt it wiser to work for them by rather subtler means.

It is here that one further internal factor came in. There were those in the Quai d'Orsay who were willing to say to all who were willing to hear that British entry would be a major setback for France. The spirit of Couve de Murville and the routine of those who had spent a decade in blocking British entry and were not eager to stand on their heads at this stage were factors in the situation. The 'professional Bruxellois' of the Quai and elsewhere knew their dossiers and were well able to look after themselves. As late as early summer 1971 one of them (unnamed) still got himself reported in *Le Monde* as hoping that if an agreement could be reached in Brussels, it would be thrown out in Westminster. Of course these men were civil servants and not political masters. But their zeal for a tough negotiation came in very useful to the Elysée. So they were given their head – and they enjoyed themselves in the bargaining right up to May 1971.

We shall examine the negotiations as a self-contained system and a procedure for settling minor issues of a transitional character in the next chapter. What matters for the purposes of the only real decision – whether the negotiations were to succeed or not – is not the subjects they were overtly about, but the time they took, the impression they gave outside, and the covert mutual signals of a political content that were contained in the economic and financial haggling.

'I am now an expert on the Barbados and Fiji sugar harvests', one negotiator could justly claim. Obviously all these tonnages were irrelevant. But 'we put up cases just to show how clever we are'. Pompidou himself could tease Maurice Schumann in public about how he seemed to enjoy being bogged down in tedious negotiations in Brussels. The negotiation as a ritual warrior dance behind which the real decisions could be considered, postponed, and finally agreed was a concept almost explicitly understood on both sides. Mr Rippon's frequent remark that the real issues could all be settled over coffee and cognac (unfortunate though its phrasing was in the British domestic context) pointed to the same apparent triviality and relative irrelevance to the core issue of much of the discussion. Rippon's initial offer of 2·6–3% of the budget for the first year and the French demand for 21·5% or more were alike symbolic stances. Pompidou's television address in January 1971 in which he referred to the 3% offer, saying that the British had 'a sense of humour, realism and tenacity – so far we have seen only the sense of humour' were all part of this posturing – as were Geoffrey Rippon's calculated losses of temper. All this ritual was reminiscent of nothing so much as Konrad Lorenz' geese.

Nevertheless there remained a very real danger that the negotiations might have developed their own negative momentum, and that by misjudgment on one side or the other they could have led to a result that neither side really wanted. No one knew exactly what limits there were on the possible terms compatible with a successful outcome. Terms acceptable to one British government might not prove acceptable to another or to Parliament, and terms acceptable to Parliament in one set of political circumstances might not prove acceptable in another. Moreover, specific terms acceptable to the French government in one political climate might not be acceptable in another – much could depend on the overtones of the British candidature. It would therefore be absurd to say that as of May 1968 or November 1968, or April 1969, or December 1969, the battle was really all over bar the shouting. On the contrary, there was no knowing whether there would be any possible overlap at the crucial moment between these two essentially still undefined and indeed elastic areas of terms acceptable to either side. Certainly, at the end of 1970 and in early 1971 there was little sign of any viable agreement in Brussels.

3   The Negotiators Dig In

It was all a gigantic irrelevance
        Conference Diplomat

The Form of the Negotiations

The legal basis of the negotiation was provided by Article 237 of the EEC treaty:

Any European State may apply to become a member of the Community. It shall address its application to the Council, which shall act unanimously after obtaining the opinion of the Commission. The conditions of admission and the adjustments to this Treaty necessitated thereby shall be the subject of an agreement between the Member States and the applicant State.

This agreement shall be submitted for ratification by all the contracting States in accordance with their respective constitutional requirements.

The Euratom Treaty has an identical article (205), and the Coal and Steel Community a corresponding one (98).

On the side of the applicants, while on 9 August 1961 Harold Macmillan had applied only for negotiations 'with a view to joining the Community if satisfactory arrangements can be made to meet the special needs of the United Kingdom, of the Commonwealth, and of the European Free Trade Association', on 10 May 1967 Harold Wilson had applied actually to join:

The Prime Minister   10, Downing Street,
                                                            Whitehall
                                                       May 10th 1967

Mr President,

    I have the honour, on behalf of her Majesty's Government in the United Kingdom of Great Britain and Northern Ireland, to inform your Excellency that the United Kingdom hereby applies to become a member of the European Economic Community under the terms of Article 237 of the treaty establishing the European Economic Community.

    Please accept, Mr President, the assurance of my highest consideration.

                                                   HAROLD WILSON

His Excellency Monsieur R. van Elslande, chairman of the Council of Ministers of the European Economic Community.

Similar applications had been made in May 1967 by Denmark, Eire and Norway. It was these four applications on which, in December 1967, 'there was not, at the present stage, agreement in the Council on continuing the procedure'.[1] Two years later, the Hague summit opened up the chance of agreement between the Six on how to proceed: and the first six months of 1970 thus saw the preparations for the negotiation to open.

At the first British attempt to negotiate entry into the Community, there had been a Conference between the Six member states of the Community and the applicant states. The Commission of the EEC, that of Euratom, and the High Authority of the Coal and Steel Community had the right to speak, and had acted as advisers to the Six in their attempts so far as possible to put common positions to the candidate countries. It had not been a very tidy form of organization. Not only had it provoked a good many accusations that the candidate countries had attempted to split the Six and to exploit differences of view between them: it had also given the candidate countries every opportunity to do so. The British and the other candidates, for their part, had found the free-for-all multilateralism of the proceedings confusing and unhelpful. Neither side wanted to return to this configuration eight years later.

Already in the Hague communiqué what was envisaged was a negotiation not between the candidates and the Six, but between the candidates and the Community. That formula, however, still left open just who would represent the Community. The French, at first sight surprisingly, seemed to favour giving this task to the Commission – an institution which it had for so long been French policy to disparage. The British on the other hand feared that this could lead to a belittling of the negotiations and leave it open for any member state later to repudiate a bargain struck between the candidates and the Commission – so that agreements reached in Brussels might then remain binding on the candidates, but not on each of the Six, any one of whom might later demand stiffer terms. It was the British view – no doubt with all due respect to the Commission – that they did not want to talk to the monkey if they could deal with the organ-grinders themselves.

In fact the Community was still agreed that since Article 237 placed the final responsibility on the member states, it was the Council of Ministers which had to negotiate. But in order to avoid the multi-

[1] Communiqué of 19 December 1967, reprinted in *The Second Try*, ed. cit., p. 319.

lateralism of 1961–63, it was decided that the member states should be represented *vis-à-vis* the four candidate states not individually, as in 1961–63, but through the President of the Council of Ministers. The representatives of the member states would be present at the confrontations with the candidates, but only as silent observers. What the President of the Council was to put to the candidates, however, was to be decided by the Council according to its normal procedures – very largely on the proposals of the Commission.

The result for the formal mechanism was obvious: the President of the Council could read to the candidates a carefully drafted compromise formula evolved between the Six, but he could hardly ever respond spontaneously to any declaration made by the candidates that did not accept the Community's terms: he had to adjourn the proceedings so that the Six could agree a new formula in every new situation. The candidate delegations – each national delegation in turn, never the four together – would sit at the bottom of the long table, perhaps listen to a series of declarations from the President of the Council (which bored the other five to tears since they, after perhaps hours of haggling over the wording, knew it only too well) and then either 'take note' or 'accept' the declaration. (The latter was sometimes possible straightaway, particularly if the candidates had already seen the declaration and been able to ascertain to their satisfaction that it lay within their negotiating positions.) They would read their own statements and, unless they had already managed to obtain prior approval informally, would then withdraw to play bridge or poker on the floor below while the meeting transformed itself upstairs into the Council of Ministers, until the Conference was reconvened by their being asked upstairs to listen to the new agreed position of the Six. The bulk of the formal negotiation was thus in a sense carried on not so much between each candidate and the six member states, but amongst the Six themselves on how (and how far) to meet the differing requirements of the four applicants. Certainly the Six spent far more of the formal sessions talking to each other than talking to the applicant states.

It will give an idea of the style of the hectic all-night negotiations simply to summarize the meetings on 29–30 November 1971 which together made up the 177th Council meeting, the 12th Conference of the Ministers with the United Kingdom, the 8th Conference with Ireland and Norway, and the 7th with Denmark. The Council of Ministers met at 11.00 a.m. on the 29th to hear the Commissioner responsible for the negotiations, Jean-François Deniau, report on the

contacts he had had with the candidate countries since the previous
meeting of the Council, and the Council decided that a new proposal
must be put forward along certain lines. After lunch the Council met in
a highly restricted session to agree on such a proposal. At 7.40 p.m. the
Ministers met with the Irish, at 8.00 p.m. with the Danes, at 8.30 p.m.
with the Norwegians – the problems on the agenda including (over
and above fisheries) taxes on table wines in Denmark, veterinary legislation in Ireland, and Norwegian agriculture. At 9.05 p.m. the British
were called in, and Geoffrey Rippon, apart from some holding statements on Papua and New Guinea, the Channel Islands and the Isle
of Man, objected to the Community's proposals on fish and on
veterinary legislation.

So the Council of Ministers had another meeting, starting at twenty
minutes past midnight. Deniau reported on his talks, held in the meantime, with the candidates' delegations: the Norwegians wanted the
twelve-mile limit for the whole of their west coast, Ireland wanted
special rules not merely for salmon and shellfish, but also for herring,
the British had now prepared a written reply with alternative counter-
proposals, including a ten-year review clause, and Geoffrey Rippon
was very anxious to get agreement before the night was out. (He hoped
that Jean-François Deniau would be able to sell the proposed review
clause to the Six – but in vain.) Jean-Marc Boegner had, however,
received telephone instructions from Maurice Schumann that in view
of the gap between positions it was not worth trying to reach agreement just then – 'not tonight'.

The British were, therefore, called in again at 2.50 a.m. Geoffrey
Rippon refused to give up and urged that at least some progress should
be made then and there – citing the bitterness on the issue in the United
Kingdom, the circumstances under which the fishing regulations had
been agreed between the Six (six hours after the opening of negotiations
with the candidates), and insisting that this question could not just be
treated as a normal transitional measure. Twenty-five minutes later the
Council was back in session, and authorized Deniau to go and talk to
the British again. At 4.40 a.m. the Norwegians came back, without any
agreement materializing between them and the Community. Ten
minutes later the Council heard a report from Deniau on his talk
with Rippon, who still wanted either a twelve-mile limit for 95% of
the coastline, or a ten-year period that was 'neither transitional nor
permanent'. The Dutch and Germans hoped it would be possible to
meet the British, but Boegner stood firm. At 6.15 a.m., still before

dawn, the Conference started again, with Geoffrey Rippon back in the room, to be told by the Italian chairman that there really was no point in going on – he himself had to leave Brussels that afternoon. But Geoffrey Rippon again insisted on a last try, and Aldo Moro agreed that the Council should meet one more time, after a few hours' interruption (for a bath, a shave and a rest) in the late morning.

So the Ministers met again at 11.30 a.m. The Commission had some suggestions ready which it had discussed at Deputy level with the British delegation between 7.00 and 8.00 a.m. and of which the Italian chairman had been informed – but the French seized the initiative by presenting an amendment of their own, which was immediately adopted. (This amendment made explicit the need for unanimity in the review of the fishing situation after the first ten years.) At 12.40 the British were called in; they felt unable to accept the new formula. At one o'clock the Irish also rejected the latest version. At 1.10 the Council, alone again, heard various Ministers vent their impatience and demand that after all the effort the Six had put into trying to accommodate the candidates, it was now up to the candidates to try to find a formula acceptable to the Six. Having followed their timetable through these twenty-six hours, one can see why at that stage the atmosphere should not have been all sweetness. But then at least they were, by November 1971, almost at the end of their task.

Of course not all problems were treated at the ministerial level. There were only thirteen ministerial meetings of the Conference throughout the negotiations. At the outset they sometimes lasted a bare ten minutes; at 'the crunch', they could go on intermittently for several days. Far more frequent were the meetings at the level of the Ministers' Deputies – the Permanent Representatives of the Six in Brussels, on whom a great deal of the real work of decision-making had come to fall in the fifteen years of the Community's existence. Their role within the Community as Permanent Representatives of the member states was formally recognized in the Treaty signed in Brussels in 1965 which established a single Council of Ministers and a single Commission for the three European Communities. Now, in the negotiations for the Communities' enlargement, they were for the first time given a task that went beyond that of preparing the meetings of the Ministers themselves: as the Ministers' Deputies they were part of the Conference when they met with the British delegation (headed at that level by Sir Con O'Neill) and with the delegations of the other candidates, to conduct negotiations on behalf of the Ministers on mandates which the Ministers themselves did not actually have to have approved in advance. With thirty-eight meetings in the eighteen months or less of serious negotiations, it is obvious that they really were crucial to the progress of the whole negotiation.

The chairman of the Committee of Permanent Representatives, and hence of the Conference meeting at that level, was the representative of the country that occupied the chair in the Council of Ministers for the half-year in question: in the latter half of 1970 under the German Foreign Minister Walter Scheel, his Permanent Representative to the Communities Ambassador Hans-Georg Sachs; in the crucial first half of 1971 under Maurice Schumann, Ambassador Jean-Marc Boegner; in the second half of 1971 (tying up left-over problems and supervising the actual treaty drafting) under the Italian Foreign Minister Aldo Moro, Ambassador Giorgio Bombassei. In many ways it was a helpful accident that the French held the presidency during the most critical stages of the negotiations, being institutionally committed to both the fairness and the success of the proceedings just when it mattered most.

In fact it was during the period when Maurice Schumann was President of the Council that the Committee of Permanent Representatives, deputizing for the Ministers, was itself supplemented by a new forum, the Committee of Deputies' Deputies – those men (second in rank in each Permanent Representation) who had specialized in the problems of the Community's enlargement (as against the many other problems which were simultaneously on the Community's agenda). All the problems, including the minor, but not for that reason always politically innocuous ones, were brought up in that body from the time of its establishment in January 1971.

In the early summer of 1971 and again later in the year, it met several times a week to prepare the meetings of the Permanent Representatives, who themselves met up to three days a week both to solve the problems assigned to them and to prepare the meetings of the Ministers. It was a three-decker system that was itself fed by reports from expert groups studying specific problems, and of course by the proposals of the Commission. At the very outset of the negotiations the British had proposed that there should also be multilateral working parties to clear the ground: but the specific subjects they proposed for such working parties met with some opposition, since there were fears that the multilateral clearing of the ground might so easily spill over into, or at least predetermine, actual negotiation. In the end tariff quotas and the final drafting of the Treaty were dealt with on this basis.

So much for the formal mechanism with its three layers. It was more than the tip of the iceberg, but a good deal less than the whole of the structure of the negotiation. For there was also a fourth level – and that in many ways by far the most important one for finding the technical solutions without which even the political will could not have come to any speedy fruition. This was the whole network of the private, informal contacts between members of different delegations, and above all between the Commission's own negotiating task force and each of the national delegations – particularly those of the applicants. This intensive dialogue between the Commission, sitting at the heart of the spider's web, and the national delegations, was a continuous process that started well before the formal opening of negotiations and often continued well after some particular decision had been formally reached.

One of the most time-consuming parts of the proceedings were the preparatory discussions between the Six and the Commission in the first half of 1970, in which the Community defined its negotiating position *vis-à-vis* the candidates' interests – which they were, of course, at that stage already forced to study in detail with the help of the candidates' representatives in Brussels. Where Britain was concerned, the cardinal document remained George Brown's presentation to Western European Union of 4 July 1967, which had raised virtually every problem that was to come up in the negotiations save fish – and that fell under the paragraph dealing with further developments in the Community.[1] And the Commission had, in September that year, sent the Council its detailed Opinion on the problems involved.[2] But the Community had evolved further in the intervening years, and the British economy also had changed; so there was a good deal more work to be done before the Six were agreed on the lines to take in the negotiation.

Once those negotiations had begun, it was again in unofficial off-the-record conversations that the ground was prepared for solutions fed one way or another (and often in alternative versions) into the formal machinery. It was here that the continuity of the process of paring down differences, trying out this formula and that, and the sense of a common intellectual enterprise were at their most marked – and in sharpest contrast to the political tactics, the sullen deadlocks and the sudden visible breakthroughs on the ministerial level at the other

[1] Cmnd 3345, reprinted in full in *The Second Try*, ed. cit., pp. 189–203.
[2] Reprinted in translation, ibid., pp. 205–99. The Commission had sent the Council a Supplementary Opinion on 1 October 1969 – before the Hague summit.

end of the scale. It was in such contacts that officials explored the complications of integrating solutions for four candidate countries in four rather different situations. It was by these means that, as early as the autumn of 1970, difficulties over liquid milk and pork meat could be settled with the British at the request of the Six in talks with the Commission.

In so far as the bulk of the matters covered in the three hundred pages of the Accession Treaty could be settled quietly on a technical level, while the really contentious issues take up only a few pages, the bulk of the negotiation clearly took place without the Ministers ever really having to sit and deliberate on them. Moreover, even the dramatically publicized political solutions never came out of the blue: they needed both careful technical preparation and discreet unofficial soundings before they were tabled. In these senses one may say that practically the whole of the negotiation took place outside the formal meetings – through exchanges of memoranda, in inter-office visits, over meals and late-night drinks, even over the telephone. We shall be dealing in the next chapter with one of the most crucial links in the process – which happened, indeed, to be forged right outside the Brussels framework. Within Brussels the network of contacts was so thick that, even if most of it did not inevitably escape the dragnet of the historian, it would be of limited interest to the general reader.

What matters is the overall character of the negotiation, and the types of role played in it by different actors. The set meetings registered agreement and acted as a formal court of appeal where agreement required major substantive differences to be resolved. For the rest – as is so often the case with any kind of set meeting the world over – their function was to act as a catalyst for the 'real' thinking and bargaining behind the scenes. They were no less important for that. But at least the formal bilateralism, cumbrous as it may have seemed, was made tolerable by this complementary set of constant contacts at various levels which anticipated the reactions of either side, and while the legal channels of communication were safeguarded by the Conference framework, these informal exchanges speeded up the work and made an effective meeting of minds possible behind the bargaining postures.

The Delegations

The key delegations in the whole process were clearly the French and the British. Willy Brandt personally and his government constituted a useful fleet-in-being that had to be reckoned with by the French and that could have set sail had it become necessary. But they were not anxious for a row with the French, and for the rest they could really take it easy: after all, whatever the terms for Britain, Germany was getting two tangible national advantages out of the Community's enlargement and the consequent arrangements for the rest of EFTA: the British, Scandinavian and, in particular, the Swiss and Austrian markets for her industry, and a lessening of her share in the burden of Community finance.

Very helpful were the Italians, who were weary of Franco-German hegemony in the Community, and saw Britain's entry, quite apart from its general foreign policy and economic impact, as a way of re-opening the political alignments within the Community. The Dutch, led in the earlier stages by Joseph Luns, were both staunchly in favour of British entry and also, on bread and butter (or rather, fish and tomato) issues, stubborn defenders of their own interests. The Belgians and Luxemburgers did their bit, Pierre Harmel, the Belgian Foreign Minister, very effectively standing up to the French on the budget contribution in May 1971. But of course there were individual differences within national delegations, and agreements and alliances that went across national demarcations.

There was in fact a good deal more overall cohesion between the six member states this time than ten years before; all six for example rejected the British proposal for an 'initiation period' before progressive transition to full membership, and all six found the opening bid for the British budget contribution derisory. But there were big issues over which the British at times felt very conscious of an underlying difference of attitude between the French and the 'friendly five': and the French, however the others might regard them, felt themselves cast in a special role.

The French negotiators saw the other five delegations as in some sense parasites on themselves: the other five had the easy job of being nice to the British, or sitting and watching the proceedings, knowing that the French would fight their battles for them against Britain's attempts at subversion of the Community and against British special interests. It was left to Maurice Schumann at the level of the Ministers (until he became chairman), to Jean-Pierre Brunet, and to Jean-Marc Boegner to stand up against the British and the other candidates in what was for much of the time a dialogue between the two delegations, conducted through an intermediary chairman of the Council before five silent spectators.

The French were well equipped for this purpose. In Jean-Marc Boegner they had a powerful figure who had played a key role in Brussels for a decade, exercised great influence on his fellow Permanent Representatives, and knew his way about. Moreover – in contrast, for example, to his German colleague – he was backed by a 'mission control' in Paris that ironed out inter-ministerial disagreements in Paris instead of letting them erupt, possibly even in front of the other countries, in Brussels itself. He received his instructions not so much from the Quai d'Orsay as from the Secretary-General of the Inter-Ministerial Committee for European Co-operation, Jean-René Bernard, who was in a key position astride three major elements in the French government – instructing Foreign Ministry personnel while combining a position in the Prime Minister's office with a post in the Elysée on the President's staff. This Inter-Ministerial Committee is a vital piece of machinery worthy of serious study as a model in Britain. It clearly gives the French a major advantage over, for instance, the Germans, whose different Ministries – and sometimes Ministers – at times appear in the European arena with openly conflicting policies.

Jean-Marc Boegner, the son of the well-known head of the French Protestant church, Pastor Marc Boegner, was regarded in Brussels as a tough character, and not necessarily friendly to the British. He had after all negotiated against them under President de Gaulle's instructions for many years. By contrast his titular boss, Maurice Schumann, was known to be friendly: he tended to explain himself at length if a British proposal was unacceptable to his government – which Jean-Marc Boegner did not always feel it necessary to do. Gaul being divided, as is well known, into fifty million Frenchmen, the French delegation was of course no more monolithic on the personal level than any other, and tensions between the French Foreign Minister and his aides, and between Jean-Marc Boegner and his mission control, became visible on more than one occasion. But then they had a difficult task during all the months when Paris appeared to have no policy beyond tough negotiating tactics, and the French representatives were left building up and defending 'holding positions' that were occasionally less disturbing than they might have been only because they were so extreme.

The British delegation was led for a brief spell – for the opening session and one ministerial meeting – by Anthony Barber. Then the accident of Iain Macleod's death catapulted Barber into the Chancellorship, and Geoffrey Rippon took over the European negotiations. An almost flamboyant, physically indefatigable, self-made Conservative

QC and businessman, Rippon's first experience of West European integration had come before he was an MP, through the Strasbourg meetings of the Council of European Municipalities. (He had been leader of the Conservatives on the LCC at the age of 33.)

Geoffrey Rippon certainly distinguished himself and commanded enormous limelight in the subsequent negotiations. If some thought that he was occasionally not persistent enough, or appeared to lose his temper for too long or with excessive publicity (and then had to swallow what he had just spat back at the Six), these are differences of view on the art of diplomacy in which no one can really calculate what the detailed outcome of a different personal style might have been. In London, though the Prime Minister himself of course followed things closely, the ministerial group to which Rippon reported and which acted as his overlord was presided over by the Foreign Secretary and included the Chancellor, the Secretary of State for Trade and Industry and the Minister of Agriculture, with Lord Carrington and William Whitelaw also very much concerned on the side of domestic political management.

Geoffrey Rippon was backed by a hand-picked civil service team that won little but praise on the Continent. Sir Con O'Neill – who had withdrawn for a time from the Foreign Office after a well-documented disagreement with George Brown over his not being appointed ambassador in Bonn – could be judicious, smooth and tenacious in excellent German and French (though in the formal negotiations he spoke in English). He had already served as British ambassador to the EEC in 1963–65, and had an excellent understanding of the workings of the Community. His deputy, John Robinson, had been one of Edward Heath's lieutenants in the 1961–63 negotiations, and had remained at the desks dealing with Britain's relations with the EEC ever since. His competence, hard work and ingenuity earned him the highest praise from the other delegations and the staff of the Commission. Sir William Nield of the Cabinet Office was clearly very influential. The Treasury was represented by Raymond Bell, the Board of Trade (Department of Trade and Industry) by Roy Denman, the Ministry of Agriculture by Freddy Kearns; technology was represented by Patrick Shovelton, while Ian Sinclair was again – as ten years before – legal adviser, and James Mellon acted as the Secretary to the Delegation.

In contrast to the team that had to go in and bat in 1961 supported by a Permanent Delegation that had moved to Brussels for the first

time only a year or less before, in 1970 there was a much greater understanding of how the Community in fact operated – and also quite a few
by then long-established personal links which made mutual compre-
hension that much easier. In the event the secret official history which
Edward Heath and his team had written of the 1961–63 negotiations did
not prove all that useful this time round.

Sir James Marjoribanks was British ambassador to the Communities
until the spring of 1971, and after an interregnum his post was filled in
the autumn by Michael Palliser from the Paris embassy. Kenneth
Christophas, who headed the Permanent Delegation during the interregnum, was in charge of dealing with all the secondary legislation – a
mammoth task of translation in the widest sense of the term, not only
linguistically but in terms of concepts, of adaptation to British circumstances, and often of very complicated transitional measures between
all the Ten. But it would be tedious to mention all who contributed to
the whole negotiation. Sir William Nield, Sir Con O'Neill and
Christopher Soames were awarded the GCMG in the New Year's
Honours List of 1972; one of their typists became an MBE. Others no
doubt will be obtaining promotion in accordance with the talents and
efforts they deployed.

For the Commission, at ministerial level, Franco-Maria Malfatti
intervened himself regularly, but the main burden was borne by Jean-
François Deniau, a French career diplomat. In his early thirties at the
time of the 1961–63 negotiations, he had even then played a key role on
the Commission's staff for those talks. Tall, elegant, smooth and clever,
he had been French ambassador to Mauritania from 1963 to 1966,
between leaving the staff of the Commission and returning to Brussels
as a Commissioner himself. His French colleague Raymond Barre was
– perhaps wrongly – considered less friendly to enlargement. A more
committed Gaullist, he was particularly in charge of the financial
and monetary aspects of the problem, and thus not unnaturally concerned to provide for all possible measures to minimize future difficulties
with monetary and economic union arising out of the special position
of the pound sterling. In the end he was to find that his tough position
on the issue had been sold out behind his back by President Pompidou
himself. With Deniau, on the other hand, there was much more of a
sense of dedication to making the negotiations succeed if that were
possible. He played much more of an intermediary's role – dining with
Edward Heath and several Ministers and their wives at Chequers in
January 1971, warning the British against their intransigent opening

bid on Community finance, reporting back to Paris on reactions, and scuttling up and down between the conference room of the Council of Ministers and the suite of offices of the British delegation, suggesting drafts and amendments to drafts. At the level of the Deputies, it was Edmund Wellenstein, a slightly older Dutchman, whose human warmth complemented Deniau's cool intellectual approach and who worked indefatigably and unreservedly for success. There are those who say that without Edmund Wellenstein – as without several other key figures not necessarily in the public limelight – the job could never have been done. Deniau and Wellenstein were in their turn assisted by a task force drawn from the various Directorates-General of the Commission, selected according to their knowledge and abilities rather than their rank, some of whom worked themselves to exhaustion in the first half of 1971 and again in the final phases preceding the signature of the Treaty of Accession.

Problems of Open Diplomacy

One of the problems with Brussels was the publicity of the proceedings. In principle they were always private. But the principle was far removed from the practice. For a start there were far too many people in the room for there to be any chance of keeping very much confidential. Moreover, since there were in effect eight participating parties, the delegations each had an interest in making sure that no one else leaked a distorted version of their stand, and usually, what is more, had an interest in leaking a (sometimes slightly coloured) version themselves. This is a phenomenon only too familiar to observers of, for example, Commonwealth conferences. But while Commonwealth conferences are episodic, and covered largely by an *ad hoc* purely temporary assemblage of journalists from all five continents, the Council of Ministers in Brussels, one way or another, sat almost as permanently as a parliament, and was covered by a permanent corps of Brussels lobby correspondents who could co-operate much more easily than lobby correspondents inside any one country: they were not so much in competition with one another as complementary to one another. It tended to take no more than half an hour after a meeting on the fifteenth floor for the Brussels press corps on the ground floor to have pieced together the essentials of the argument and the prevailing atmosphere from rival accounts given by members of different delegations. From the outset, therefore, everyone realized that few things could be kept really secret for very long. (It was, of course, hopeless to ask the press to keep anything out of the papers, though there were moments when the British delegation was thankful that journalists' researches had not progressed as far as they might have done.)

Given this inevitable instant publicity, it was decided that the Chairman of the Council and the British Minister should give a joint press conference after each meeting at the ministerial level on what had (and had not) been achieved at each stage. The result was a form of semi-open diplomacy, tempered by the discreet network of informal contacts, but still a very much more complex task than the conclusion of open agreements secretly arrived at. For the sake of appearances, quite apart from the negotiating logic itself, each successive stage in the process of reaching agreement thus had to be represented as a fair component package between the participants within what it was hoped would ultimately be a fair overall package deal: and that demand for internal symmetry of the parts as well as of the whole imposed its own limitation on the negotiations and invited deadlock, with neither side prepared to make the first move.

The British delegation, in particular, faced a thorny dilemma. If their opening bid was not very high (or their opening offer not very low) they were immediately accused at home of selling the pass before the battle had even begun. If their opening bid was high (or their offer low), they knew they were liable to have to depart from it, and be accused of having lost the battle. On the whole, they opted for something nearer the second horn of the dilemma, bargained hard from positions quite some way removed from the likely final outcome, and hoped that public opinion at home understood that these were bargaining positions and would not, when the final package came to be tied up, measure their 'betrayal of the national interest' by the distance they had had to go to meet the Six half way.

Thus the British delegation had, as we saw, on 16 December made its opening bid for Britain's share in the gross contributions to the Community budget with a figure of 2·6-3·0% for the first year – perhaps the only time it made a totally unreasonable demand. The stalemate over that issue was to last for months, by which time the British press itself had begun telling the government not to be silly and to come off it: when Geoffrey Rippon, six months later, accepted the figure of 8·64% for the first year, sufficient time had passed and quite enough other issues had taken the limelight for the government to be able to slide off that particular hook without too much trouble.

Perhaps slightly more embarrassing in some ways were the apparent turns and turn-abouts over sugar in May 1971, when Geoffrey Rippon first had the word spread that he had used very tough language to the Six, demanded that this 'dialogue of the deaf must end', and insisted on stronger guarantees being written into the Treaty – when he had nearly got the whole of his negotiating objective. The need to play to the gallery here included not only the audience in Westminster but also that in Suva, Kingston, Port-of-Spain and Port Louis. It was hardly surprising if the public at home and overseas took it, after such language, that the terms finally agreed were unsatisfactory: for only a few hours later Geoffrey Rippon accepted a formula that differed but little from the previous one, and certainly contained no reference to sugar quantities, prices, or even to the sugar industries themselves. (The British negotiators had in fact long ago abandoned the idea of getting any such price and quantitative guarantees into the Treaty.) The negotiators of the Six recall that, later that night (too late to catch next morning's headlines at home), Geoffrey Rippon came close to apologizing for his earlier outburst.

Autonomous factors of public opinion on the general principle of entry also, of course, entered as a factor into the negotiations. The deterioration in the British opinion polls on the question did not go unmarked in Brussels. To some extent it could help the British delegation to point to all the opposition they would have to face at home and argue that entry was only possible if the terms were better – the old use of a government's domestic weakness as a source of diplomatic strength. When they really had to get a big concession from the Six, then the openness of the diplomacy could be a useful card to play. At the same time the timetable of British domestic politics imposed pressures on the negotiation. The Prime Minister was determined not to lose momentum and to have the agreement sewn up in all essentials before the summer recess and before the economic situation, Ireland, Rhodesia or other untoward factors could sour the climate at home.

While these problems were shared by the Irish, Danes and Norwegians, each of whom were to face referenda at home after the full terms were known, it weighed very little on the delegations of the member states themselves. Their publics were generally in favour of the Communities' enlargement, so any concessions could be justified on those grounds: perhaps it was only the French beet-sugar producers who ever really appealed to the public for any particular safeguards against the possible consequences of entry. Though the French delegation occasionally claimed to be under pressure from their farmers, there was little evidence that this presented any real threat to their freedom of manœuvre – and the French press was not used more than might have been expected of it to entrench the delegation in any particular position. In any case, the enlargement of a Community in which one has already lived for over a decade is a much less dramatic event than entering one from the outside – particularly when it has evolved according to its own requirements for fourteen years, and will deeply affect vast areas of national life. So, apart from some specialists and dedicated Europeans, there was substantially less public interest in these negotiations on the Continent than in the applicant states.

The Start of the Marathon

Luxemburg really figures as the fourth city in our tale, for it was here that the negotiations formally began and here, a year later, that the biggest of all its 'crunches' took place. Indeed, both the place and the date of the opening of the negotiations were meant to be significant. Luxemburg had housed the Coal and Steel Community and also several of the joint Community institutions after the EEC and Euratom were set up; when a single Council and Commission were established for all three Communities (parallel with the single European Parliament that watches over all three), it was agreed that Luxemburg should still be the venue for Council meetings in April, June and October. Since it had been informally agreed at The Hague that the negotiations should open before the first half-year was out, the date was fixed for 30 June, and the place therefore Luxemburg.

The formation of a new British government only eight days before might have been a reasonable cause for postponement: but Edward Heath deliberately stuck to the pre-arranged date. He was determined that there should be no delay on Britain's side: the nearer to his election victory it could all be achieved, the greater would his standing – not to use the word mandate – be on this as on other issues. He was also determined that there should be no excuse later for delay on the side of the Six. Besides, the Labour government had prepared a dossier for the opening of negotiations which the Conservative government could pick up as it stood. Anthony Barber's opening speech in Luxemburg was based on the draft prepared for George Thomson. There was no need to change the civil service team that had been formed to negotiate under a Labour government. The negotiating positions, optimal and fall-back, did not have to be changed because of the general election result. Britain was going through a period of European bipartisanship, and the new government could simply carry on where the old one had left off.

The Luxemburg meeting was, of course, formal in one sense, but its purpose was far more than that of taking a 'family photograph'. The two set speeches, Barber's and Harmel's, clearly set out the opening positions on both sides. Barber's was on the whole very well received, though one friend of British entry wrote afterwards: 'One quickly saw that he knew neither his dossier nor the continent. He regaled his audience with a very dry, very cautious, rather pretentious little speech, giving the impression it was jolly good of Britain to go in with the Six.'[1] Granted Anthony Barber was not identical with George Brown, such criticism was not, however, really fair. There had been another veto in the meantime, and quite apart from a somewhat negative British public opinion listening in, the reservations expressed in Barber's speech were not merely a bargaining posture, they were also all too true; and he certainly rehearsed at length the reasons why Britain felt she must now join the Communities (and thereby acknowledged how wrong she had been in the 'fifties). Like George Brown in 1967, he accepted the Treaties, their political objectives, and the legislation made under them in full, only defining the exact problems on which Britain had special requirements for the transition period.

Pierre Harmel, for the Community, set out its position:

A. We assume in principle that your states accept the treaties and their political objectives, all the decisions of every type which have been taken since the treaties came into force and the choices made in the field of development.

These decisions also include the agreements concluded by the Community with third countries.

B. Under these conditions, the Community wishes at the opening of the negotiations to state a certain number of principles which it intends to apply:

1. The rule which must necessarily govern the negotiations is that the solution of any problems of adjustment which may arise must be sought in the establishment of transitional measures and not in changes in the existing rules.

2. The object of the transitional measures will be to allow for the adjustments which prove to be necessary as a consequence of the enlargement. Their duration must be restricted to that required to achieve this aim. As a general rule, they must incorporate detailed timetables and must commence with an

[1] Anne Laurens, *L'Europe avec les Anglais*, Arthaud, Paris, 1971, p. 217.

initial significant mutual tariff reduction on the entry into force of the accession treaties.

3. The transitional measures must be conceived in such a way as to ensure an overall balance of reciprocal advantages.

With this in mind, it will be necessary to ensure an adequate synchronization of the progress of freedom of movement of industrial goods with the achievement of the agricultural common market.

This consideration must be taken into account in respect of the duration of the transitional measures in the industrial and agricultural sectors.

4. In the field of trade, the duration of the transitional period should be the same for all the applicants.

5. In the other fields in which transitional measures prove to be necessary, the duration of such measures could, if possible and desirable, be varied according to their subject matter and the applicants involved. These questions will be examined during the negotiations.

6. The various accession treaties should come into force on the same date.

C. It is the Community's opinion that the accession of new members will lead to the enlarged Community having new responsibilities towards developing countries, which it will have to meet in appropriate ways. . . .

In July the Conference got down to the nuts and bolts of organization, and then, in September, the real substantive work began. At the turn of the year, after three ministerial meetings and nine at the level of the Deputies, certain questions were got out of the way – though on occasion the Ministers urged the Deputies not to announce some of their agreements but to leave them for the Council to announce, so that the Ministers did not have to go to their press conferences empty-handed.

Fortunately some problems did not need any arguing about. Of course every agreement on any one issue was conditional on agreement on all other issues. Subject to that proviso, for example, Britain was to have full voting rights in the institutions from the day of her accession, even though she would not be fulfilling all the duties of membership until after the end of the transition period or periods. That meant that, like the French, Germans and Italians, Britain would have 36 members of the European Assembly, 24 seats on the Economic and Social Council, and provide two members for the Commission and two judges for the Court of Justice, as well as having the right to nominate an Advocate-General to the Court. Assuming the simultaneous accession of Denmark, Norway and Ireland, this meant enlarging the Assembly to 153, bringing the Commission back to 14, enlarging the Court to 11 judges, and so on. Most of these adjustments were pretty straightforward.